D1070363

iPhone® Photography

by Mark Hemmings

for
dummies®
A Wiley Brand

iPhone® Photography For Dummies®

Published by: **John Wiley & Sons, Inc.,** 111 River Street, Hoboken, NJ 07030-5774, www.wiley.com

Copyright © 2020 by John Wiley & Sons, Inc., Hoboken, New Jersey

Published simultaneously in Canada

For general information on our other products and services, please contact our Customer Care Department within the U.S. at 877-762-2974, outside the U.S. at 317-572-3993, or fax 317-572-4002. For technical support, please visit https://hub.wiley.com/community/support/dummies.

Wiley publishes in a variety of print and electronic formats and by print-on-demand. Some material included with standard print versions of this book may not be included in e-books or in print-on-demand. If this book refers to media such as a CD or DVD that is not included in the version you purchased, you may download this material at http://booksupport.wiley.com. For more information about Wiley products, visit www.wiley.com.

Library of Congress Control Number: 2020905587

ISBN 978-1-119-68779-5 (pbk); ISBN 978-1-119-68781-8 (ePDF); ISBN 978-1-119-68780-1 (epub)

Manufactured in the United States of America

V10019564_070720

Contents at a Glance

Table of Contents

Introduction

I n 2007, the world was stunned at a just-released futuristic device called the iPhone. A mobile phone without physical keys? There was no middle ground — either you loved it or hated it — upon seeing the iPhone advertised for the first time. Those polarizing attitudes changed quickly, however, when the public came to see the wisdom of a full touch screen.

Whether they anticipated it or not, Apple quickly realized that its new "magical device" (to quote Steve Jobs) was quickly becoming one of the world's most popular cameras! And it's easy to see why. Who wouldn't want the immediate gratification of seeing their photos instantly on a large yet pocketable screen? And to have your camera with you all the time? That's a recipe for a revolution in the world of photography.

So now it's time to turn attention to you. Maybe you're someone who feels and understands the soul of a particular place but has a challenging time with the technical side of photography. Or maybe you're the opposite, where you have always found the technical side of things easy, but you struggle with capturing emotion, mood, metaphors, and heart in your photographs. Regardless of what your challenge is, this book is well-suited to help you both master the technical and the artistic sides of iPhone photography. The technical side of the iPhone camera is actually easy to understand, which will free you up to apply creative concepts to each of your images.

About This Book

iPhone Photography For Dummies is a book written for you. No matter what level of iPhone experience you have, or what your history in photography is, the goal of this book is to get you excited about the possibility of seeing at least one iPhone photo opportunity each day! As your iPhone is almost always with you, either in your backpack, purse, schoolbag, or back pocket, you almost always have access to a surprisingly good quality camera. This book gives you the technical and creative tools that will fuel your desire to photograph pretty much daily.

In this book, I show you how to

>> Take and edit your photos in the quickest yet most accurate way possible.

>> Navigate your way around all the iPhone camera settings and options.

>> Access and use the extra camera features, such as panoramics and selfies.

>> Create the best landscape, sports, family, travel, products, and portrait photographs.

>> Apply HDR to your landscape photos for perfect exposure even in tricky light.

>> Initiate Burst mode for sports and family photography to ensure that you get the shot.

>> Utilize light in its many forms to create the best-looking subjects.

>> Apply the Rule of Thirds and other compositional tools to your images.

>> Edit, organize, and share your iPhone photos.

>> Create smooth-looking videos.

>> And plenty more!

Foolish Assumptions

In classic *For Dummies* style, this book assumes that you may know nothing about the subject matter, yet is also highly accessible and valuable to those who may consider themselves as advanced amateurs. *iPhone Photography For Dummies* gently guides you through the best practices of mobile photography, helping you gain a new creative outlet to express yourself and to impress your friends and family!

So to start you out on a path to photographic success, I assume that you

>> Have an iPhone and its iOS operating system is up-to-date.

>> You have access to Wi-Fi or use a data plan with your mobile phone provider.

>> You know your Apple iCloud account login and password so that you can upload your photos to iCloud.

Other than these three presumptions, I explain everything else in the book in great detail so that you never feel overwhelmed or bogged down.

Icons Used in This Book

This book, like all *For Dummies* books, uses icons to highlight certain paragraphs and to alert you to particularly useful information. Here's a rundown of what those icons mean:

TIP

A Tip icon means I'm giving you an extra snippet of information that may help you on your way or provide some additional insight into the concepts being discussed.

REMEMBER

The Remember icon points out information that is worth committing to memory.

TECHNICAL STUFF

The Technical Stuff icon indicates geeky stuff that you can skip if you really want to, although you may want to read it if you're the kind of person who likes to have the background info.

WARNING

The Warning icon helps you stay out of trouble. It's intended to grab your attention to help you avoid a pitfall that may harm your iPhone.

Beyond the Book

In addition to what you're reading right now, this product also comes with a free access-anywhere Cheat Sheet with fingertip facts about iPhone photography. To get this Cheat Sheet, simply go to www.dummies.com and search for "iPhone Photography For Dummies Cheat Sheet" in the Search box.

Where to Go from Here

Before you dive into the exciting world of iPhone photography, please remember that you are creative (even if you don't feel creative). Creativity is in everyone to some degree, and it's often the case that we simply need a guide to kick-start that engine. It is my hope that this book will serve that function, to help you master the technical parts which will free you up to absorb the artistic aspects of iPhone photography. I know that you can do it!

And if you are still having doubts that you can take really good photos with your iPhone, each sample photo (called a *figure*) in this book was taken by me with an iPhone.

One final word before you get to Chapter 1. Throughout this process of discovering the ins and outs of iPhone photography, take inspiration from other photographers who have mastered their preferred photographic genre. Instagram is a good resource for this. However, it's also critical that you don't allow yourself to feel bad if your photos are not up to that level. Practice creating photographs every day, if possible, and you will most certainly see your abilities radically improve over a short period of time.

1

Fast-Tracking Your Photography Skills

Chapter **1**

Introducing iPhone Photography

Phone photography is one of the most satisfying ways to express yourself, as the iPhone and its camera allow you to present your interpretation of the world to as many people as possible. And the best part is that you don't need to be represented by an art gallery or hire expensive talent agents. Simply pull the iPhone out of your pocket, take the photo that is in front of you, edit that photo to perfection, and then share your finely tuned image to the world via social media, all within one little handheld device!

Getting to Know the Camera in Your iPhone

As of this writing, Apple produces iPhones that have a single lens camera, a dual lens, and a triple lens. Understanding these hardware differences straightaway can help you navigate your own iPhone better, as well as help you with future purchasing decisions.

REMEMBER

One thing to keep in mind is that it doesn't matter if your iPhone model only has one lens. Don't ever feel that you may be left out because of your model of iPhone! Here is a truth that you can hold onto: Learning about composition, light, color, and photographic genre best practices are more important than having the latest and greatest gear. Rest assured, you'll succeed with this book regardless of your iPhone model and its age.

The following list describes which iPhone model has what lenses. Included are iPhones that are supported by iOS 13, as of this writing.

>> **Triple Ultra Wide, wide, and telephoto lens iPhone models:** 11 Pro and 11 Pro Max

>> **Dual Ultra Wide and wide angle lens iPhone models:** iPhone 11

>> **Dual wide and telephoto lens iPhone models:** Xs, Xs Max, X, 8 Plus, and 7 Plus

>> **Single lens wide angle iPhone models:** Xr, 8, 7, 6s Plus, 6s, 6 Plus, and SE

Models with one lens

The single lens iPhone has one camera that has a wide-angle view, which means that a single lens iPhone is fantastic for landscapes, travel or vacation photography, street photography, architecture, full-body portraiture, and many more genres. But that's not all . . . this lens (as with all iPhone wide angle lenses) can photograph small objects at a very close distance. Thus, it becomes a useful substitute when DSLR (large camera) photographers need to photograph something small, but don't have what are called close-up macro lenses with them.

Figure 1-1 shows an example of the out-of-production but highly regarded iPhone SE, which sports a single lens. All iPhone series earlier than the 11 models have a single lens option and are usually less expensive to purchase.

Models with two lenses

Most dual lens iPhones add what Apple calls a *telephoto view,* which means that the second additional lens has what is popularly called a *zoomed-in view.* That description is technically incorrect as the lens cannot physically zoom in and out. However, it's an adequate description in that you'll be able to see faraway objects much better by using this additional lens.

TIP

This telephoto lens is very similar to the viewing angle of your eyes. Thus, it has been a popular *field of view* for those who want an accurate display of whatever is in front of their lens.

FIGURE 1-1:
Example
of a single lens
iPhone model.

With the advent of the iPhone 11 series, the *non-Pro* dual lens models called iPhone 11 do not have a telephoto lens option. However, they can certainly zoom in with what is called *digital zoom*. Their lenses are the wide and the ultra-wide-angle versions. The triple lens iPhone 11 Pro series includes the telephoto lens as well as the two wide angle options.

Figure 1-2 is an example of what a typical two lens iPhone would look like. Keep in mind that earlier series iPhones had the two lenses side-by-side in a horizontal arrangement, while later series iPhones had the two lenses stacked vertically.

FIGURE 1-2:
The dual lens
iPhone XS Max's
wide-angle and
telephoto lenses.

Models with three lenses

With the advent of the iPhone 11 Pro models, Apple has entered the three-lens game. The new addition is called an *Ultra Wide* angle lens, and it is truly wide! You'll be able to fit in your composition a huge amount of the scene in front of you for a unique super wide view.

The Ultra Wide lens is perfect for landscape and architectural photographers, and street photographers have been putting this lens to very good use as well. The other two lenses haven't changed much with regards to the viewing angle. You'll still have the normal wide angle and telephoto view, much the same as what you would have been used to with any older dual lens iPhone models.

The iPhone 11 Pro Max and its triple lens layout is shown in Figure 1-3. However, keep in mind that the 11 Pro (which is a bit smaller in size) has the same three lenses with the same image quality.

FIGURE 1-3:
Triple lens cameras that come with the iPhone 11 Pro and 11 Pro Max models.

YOUR iPhone CAMERA VERSUS A PROFESSIONAL CAMERA

A lot of people get tempted by the allure of a very expensive professional DSLR camera, as they believe that they can create better photographs with it. While improved photographs can certainly be true, keep in mind that most photography these days is viewed on a screen. This view means that it's often difficult to judge which image is from an iPhone and which is from a pro-level DSLR when compared on a portable device.

So, the general rule is to take your iPhone camera to the furthest that you can push it. And when you feel that you have mastered the iPhone and are feeling creatively held back, then consider a DSLR or mirrorless style of camera. The larger cameras will have greater resolution, but keep in mind that they don't have the convenience of the iPhone, which often makes the iPhone a better choice for daily use.

Future models with more than three lenses

Could there ever be a four-lens iPhone model? At the time of this writing, there are only rumors. However, it wouldn't be surprising to have an additional fourth lens in the future that is even more of a telephoto view than the normal telephoto lens. While it would take a near engineering miracle to fit a longer telephoto lens on an iPhone, micro technology is advancing at such a rate that we may see such an iPhone within a short amount of time.

Taking a Quick Tour of the iPhone Camera App

As of this writing, the iPhone 11 camera screens have a slightly different look than the camera screen that you will see with any iPhone from series X models and earlier. But don't worry; this camera walk-around will still make sense to you even though the figures may look a little different than your own iPhone's camera screen. For example, Figure 1-4 shows the typical camera screen view of the iPhone XS Max, using iOS 13. If you have a single lens iPhone, such as the XR, your screen will look slightly different than Figure 1-4 due to the fact that you won't see the 1x zoom option that comes with dual lens iPhones.

The iPhone 11 series has a brand-new look, which neatens up the camera interface and has some usability improvements. This book shows examples from an iPhone 11 series model, which looks similar to Figure 1-5. Again, don't feel that you will be left out because you don't have an iPhone 11. Even though the look is slightly different, the core functionality is quite similar to previous generations of iPhones.

FIGURE 1-4: Camera screen view of an iPhone XS Max iPhone.

FIGURE 1-5:
The new camera
look introduced
on all iPhone 11
series models.

Taking a Photo

When you turn on your iPhone, you see what is called your lock screen, which looks similar to Figure 1-6. Press and hold the small camera icon at the bottom right for about 1 full second and then let go. You should now see the Camera app screen.

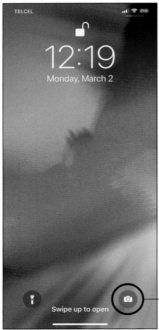

FIGURE 1-6:
A typical iPhone
lock screen.

Push and hold this camera icon
for about one full second

Alternatively, if you're already within your iPhone and you can see all your apps, simply tap on the camera icon. Figure 1-7 shows an example of the iPhone Camera app icon.

With your Camera app open, find a good scene that you want to photograph and tap the large white shutter button circle at the bottom of the screen, as shown in Figure 1-8.

FIGURE 1-7:
A highlighted screenshot showing the Camera app icon.

FIGURE 1-8:
Example of the shutter button used to take a photo.

Viewing Your iPhone Photos

After taking your photo, close the Camera app and return to your home screen. Tap your Photos app, as shown in Figure 1-9.

FIGURE 1-9:
A highlighted
screenshot
showing the
Photos app,
where your
photos are
stored.

TIP

You can actually access your photo at the bottom left of your Camera app screen. Simply tap the little square thumbnail version of your latest photo, and it will open full size for you to review.

At the bottom right of your screen, make sure you tap Albums (as shown in Figure 1-10), and then tap the Recents album at the top left of your app screen.

You can flip between all your photos using a horizontal swipe motion with your finger or thumb (see Figure 1-11).

TIP

To see greater detail in your photo, use the *pinch-to-zoom* technique. Place your index finger and thumb on your photo and then widen the space between both of your fingers to zoom in. Do the opposite to zoom out.

FIGURE 1-10:
Choose Albums,
and then Recents
to access all your
photos.

FIGURE 1-11:
Your photo
review screen.

Editing Your iPhone Photo

On the top right of your screen, tap Edit to access the photo editing tools.

At the bottom middle, tap the Auto magic wand icon, as shown in Figure 1-12. Did you see any changes in your photo?

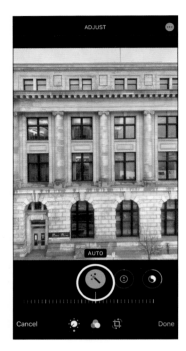

FIGURE 1-12:
Press the Auto magic wand icon for your first photo edit.

Underneath Auto are many small vertical lines that act as a type of scroll bar. As in Figure 1-13, with your finger scroll left and then right until you get your desired artistic appearance.

When done, press the yellow Done option at the bottom right of your screen.

There are so many excellent editing tools beyond this Auto feature — so many of them, in fact, that Chapter 11 is devoted to exploring each tool in depth.

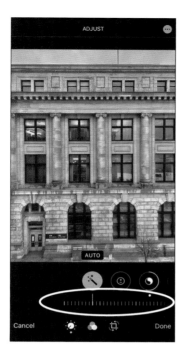

FIGURE 1-13:
The scrollable
adjustment
option for
different editing
looks.

One of the most common photo editing question from iPhone users is "Do I need to save my photo edits?" The answer is no! The Photos app will do everything for you. In fact, your photo automatically gets saved pretty much every second when you're doing editing work.

REMEMBER

Sharing Your Photos

Sharing your edited photo couldn't be easier! Tap the little up-arrow Share icon at the bottom left of your screen. (If you don't see the Share icon, tap anywhere within your photo, and it will appear.) You can now share your photo to Messages, Mail, Airdrop, and any other iOS app that supports sharing. Figure 1-14 shows what the sharing screen looks like.

FIGURE 1-14:
The sharing
screen allows you
to share your
photo using
various apps.

IN THIS CHAPTER

» Opening your camera in different ways

» Holding your iPhone properly

» Zooming in to your subject

» Photographing with the selfie camera

» Using the Live Photo feature

» Applying filters to your photos

Chapter **2**

Taking the Complete Camera Walk-Around

Your iPhone includes a surprising number of advanced features. However, the designers also tried to make the iPhone a simple device to use, which is good news for you. This ease of use allows you to quickly and easily get the shot without having to learn complex techniques.

The goal of this chapter is to help you quickly master the iPhone camera by offering you what's often called a walk-around. When you understand the layout of the camera, and what each feature does, you'll be able to act quickly when the decisive moment presents itself to you.

REMEMBER

Keep in mind that this book uses screenshots from the iPhone 11 series models. The look of the screenshots may be a bit different than your own iPhone, but the core concepts are the same. When absolutely needed, I include a screenshot from the 11 series and the X (and earlier) series models.

Discovering the Different Ways to Open Your Camera

In Chapter 1, you discover the usual method for opening the iPhone camera from both the lock screen and while navigating your apps on your home screen. You can, however, take advantage of a number of other ways to access the camera so that you can get to photographing faster:

» **Left-swipe from your lock screen:** Instead of holding the camera icon at the bottom right of your lock screen for a full second, try the right-to-left swipe, as shown in Figure 2-1. Simply put your finger slightly outside the edge of your phone on the right side and then swipe to the left. This motion opens your camera quickly for those fleeting moments!

» **Control Center camera access:** To access the Control Center, which gives you the option to open the camera app, simply swipe down with your index finger from the upper-right corner of the screen, as shown in Figure 2-2. You see a number of customizable quick-access icons. Tap the one that is shaped like a camera. If you're using an older model iPhone and/or have an older version of the iOS operating system, swipe up from the bottom edge of your screen to open the Control Center.

FIGURE 2-1:
Swipe right to left to quickly access the camera.

FIGURE 2-2:
Swipe down from the upper-right corner to access Control Center.

Properly Holding Your iPhone for Steady Photographs

Have you ever taken an iPhone photo with your arms fully extended and your iPhone as far away from your face as possible? While this posture may be the way that the majority of mobile photographers take their photos, it's not a good idea.

TIP

One of the keys to creating sharp photos is to have a stable platform for your iPhone. To provide this stability, you can use a tripod, rest your iPhone on a stable surface, or use your own steady hands. But how do you make sure that your hands and arms are steady? The answer is simple:

1. **Pull your elbows into your ribcage to stabilize your arms.**

2. **Place your iPhone as close to your face as possible, based on your level of close-sightedness.**

3. **Take a deep breath in, exhale, and when you're at the bottom of your exhale, take the photo.**

TIP

If your level of mobility allows for it, kneel to take your photo using one leg as a stabilizer.

Figures 2-3 and 2-4 give you an example of optimal postures and camera-holding positions.

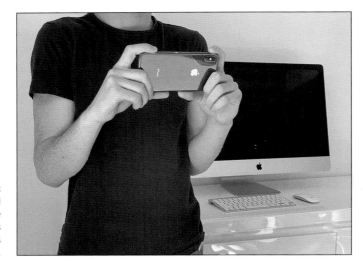

FIGURE 2-3:
Elbows pulled into your ribcage and phone as close to you as possible.

FIGURE 2-4:
Ideal kneeling position for steady photo capture.

By using these stabilizing tips each time that you take a handheld photo, you will come home with far more successfully sharp photos.

REMEMBER

A tripod is the gold standard for sharp photos from any type of camera, but you may not have one with you.

Taking a Photo Without Using the Normal Shutter Button

The majority of iPhone photos are captured by tapping the prominent large circle within the camera app. However, in some circumstances, an alternate shutter release is more advantageous. *Shutter release* is a photography term that refers to any object that tells the camera to take a photo as soon as you activate it. A shutter release may be physical, such as the volume buttons on Apple EarPods, or it may be part of an iPhone screen that requires a tap or a press of your finger.

Use the method of tripping the shutter that is most convenient and natural for you.

Side shutter using the volume buttons

With your camera app open and ready to take a photo, instead of using the normal shutter circle to take your photo, try pressing the volume buttons. Using the side shutter is a different way to capture your image, and often photographers feel that using a physical button as a shutter release is more like how they create photos using their larger DSLR cameras. Some people like the physical feedback of a push-button shutter release, and this method is a perfect alternative.

It doesn't matter if you press the volume-up or volume-down button, as both will take the photo. The volume buttons are on the side of your iPhone and have a + and - etching similar to Figure 2-5.

Apple EarPods volume controller shutter release

Apple EarPods can also act as a *shutter-release cable*. If you have a pair of Apple EarPods, all you have to do is open the camera app, plug in your EarPods, and then press either the volume-up or the volume-down button, as shown in Figure 2-6.

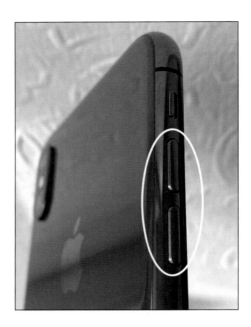

FIGURE 2-5:
Press either the +
or - volume
button to take a
photo.

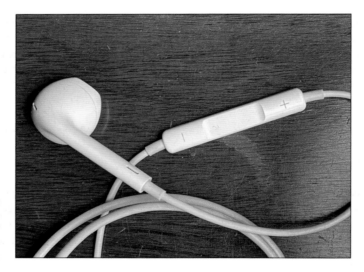

FIGURE 2-6:
Use the volume
buttons on your
EarPods to take a
photo.

TIP

This method of taking a photo is really useful for creating a super-steady photo when your iPhone is on a tripod or resting on a stable surface. It's also an easier way to press the shutter button when doing *selfie* photos (taking photos of your-self). Figure 2-7 has an example of an iPhone user taking a selfie by using the volume buttons to activate the camera. (Want more selfie tips? Check out Chapter 4!)

FIGURE 2-7:
Make it easier to
take selfies by
tapping your
EarPods' volume
buttons.

Zooming in to Your Subject

If you feel that your main subject appears too far away in your composition, you can visually bring that subject much closer to occupy more space within your picture. The term *zooming in* is borrowed from standard cameras that have lenses that can physically zoom in and zoom out. Simply stated, by the act of *zooming out* you can have a very wide looking scene where a lot is included in your photo, or you can *zoom in* to capture the plumage of a beautiful bird in a distant tree.

Originally, the ability of cameras to zoom either in or out was only done with a mechanical movement of metal and glass within the *zoom lens,* similar to the lens pictured in Figure 2-8.

With the advent of point and shoot cameras, and then mobile device cameras, such as the iPhone, *digital zooming* was made possible. Digital zoom doesn't rely on any physical movement of the camera lenses. In simplistic terms, it's an artificial expansion of pixels (millions of single bits that make up your photo) that simulates the effects of a traditional zoom lens.

The good part of digital zoom is that you can visually bring faraway objects closer within your composition. Think of that bird on a distant tree.

WARNING

Zooming in does have a downside, however. With each increase in digital zoom, the quality of the overall image decreases.

FIGURE 2-8:
Example of a
zoom lens used
on DSLR or
mirrorless style
cameras.

The designers of the various mobile device companies knew about the limitations of digital zooming, which is why they introduced dual-lens mobile device cameras. The first iPhone with two lenses was released in late 2016 and named the iPhone 7 Plus. The addition of a lens that was less wide than the normal iPhone lens allowed photographers to rely less on digital zooming when trying to see far-away objects. Picture quality quickly improved in the world of iPhone photography, no doubt because digital zooming was done less frequently.

But is digital zooming all that bad? Not really, especially with late-model iPhones. One motto that you may want to keep top of mind: "It's better to *get the shot* with technical imperfections than to miss the shot entirely."

Zooming best practices

To practice using digital zoom on one of your photos, give the following steps a try after you choose the lens that has the most telephoto view. Take a look at Figure 2-9 to see three lens views. Depending on your camera model, choose the lens that visually appears to bring distant objects closer to you. For some iPhone models, it will be called the *x2* lens, and for others the *x1* lens.

Try these easy steps with your own iPhone to practice the pinch-to-zoom technique, which allows you to view distant objects much closer.

1. **Open your camera app.**

2. **Choose the x2 lens, if possible; if not, choose the x1 lens.**

3. **Find a scene in front of you that has a distant object that you want to see closer.**

4. **Pinch your finger and thumb and place them on your screen.**

5. **Move your finger and thumb away from each other while still fully touching the screen.**

6. **Stop the digital zoom when you feel your subject is big enough within your composition.**

REMEMBER

Figure 2-10 shows examples of the finger placement needed to perform the pinch-to-zoom technique. Keep in mind that both your finger and thumb need to have constant contact with the screen during the entire zooming process, or it won't work. This pinch-to-zoom technique works for both zooming in prior to taking the photo and also afterward when you are reviewing your photo, such as what you see in Figure 2-10. The pinch-to-zoom process is identical for both taking and reviewing your photos.

FIGURE 2-10:
Initiating the
pinch-to-zoom
technique using
your thumb and
forefinger.

Cropping instead of digital zooming

The contents of Chapter 11 go into cropping in greater detail, so the following steps are simply a quick tip for alternate zooming results:

1. **Take your photo of the distant object using your most telephoto-view lens.**

2. **Open your Photos app and locate the photo you just created.**

3. **Crop your photo to the extent that you can now see that distant object much better.**

TECHNICAL
STUFF

At some point, you may hear the term *interpolation* when talking about digital zoom. Interpolation is a technical word that refers to artificially making a digital photo larger, or you could say making a photo appear to be zoomed-in much more than what the physical lens can naturally produce.

You may be wondering why anyone would crop a photo, which makes it smaller, rather than use the intelligence of the iPhone to create a realistic looking digital zoom. The answer is twofold:

>> Not too many years ago, digital zoom results were terrible! These days, they're extremely good due to advancements in image manipulation programming. However, many people remember the old days of poor quality interpolation and are still reluctant to use digital zoom.

>> Even though the cropped image is smaller in resolution size, purists would prefer to sacrifice photo size to avoid any image resizing manipulation by the iPhone's computer.

Either option is fine to get you exactly what you want in your image. Please remember, however, that the more you digitally zoom in with your finger and thumb, the harder it is for your iPhone's brain to give you a good sharp and clear image. In saying that, however, the late model iPhones do a remarkable job at what they call 10x digital zoom, which is the maximum telephoto that you can achieve on a late model iPhone.

If you have your iPhone with you right now, choose your 2x or 1x lens view and then use the pinch-to-zoom technique to zoom in to 10x to see just how far away you can photograph. Now take the photo and upon review, check out the quality of the 10x zoom photo. It's not too bad, is it? While not perfect, feel free to use digital zoom to bring those distant objects really close.

If you don't have your iPhone with you at the moment, Figure 2-11 shows just how much zoom you can achieve by using the 2x lens plus 10x digital zoom. Do you see how close the building's arches appear to be now? It's a pretty good quality photo for being so far away from the iPhone's camera.

FIGURE 2-11:
The impressive result of extending digital zoom all the way up to 10x magnification.

Using the Selfie Camera with and without Background Blur

Taking a photo of yourself with the front-facing lens on your iPhone is popularly called a *selfie*. You hold your iPhone away from your face, and then when you like the composition (how you're framed in the photo), you take the shot.

Sometimes called the *selfie-cam*, the front-facing lens on your iPhone is actually quite useful for a number of different applications. But its greatest claim to fame is getting a good shot of you! Here's how to access the front-facing camera for your next selfie, with an example of what it looks like in Figure 2-12:

1. **Open the iPhone camera app.**

2. **Tap on the intertwined arrow-circle icon at the bottom right.**

3. **When you see yourself and like the composition, take the photo.**

FIGURE 2-12:
The selfie camera
screen
appearance.

After you take your selfie and review the photo, you may feel that it's not the best-looking self-portrait that you've seen. This viewpoint is understandable, as wide-angle lenses like this one tend to distort faces to the point of looking a bit rounder and heavier than in reality. While you can't do much about the physical limitations of wide-angle camera lenses, some digital solutions do at least make your selfie look a bit more professional!

Follow these steps to activate Portrait mode, which usually does a good job of creating better-looking selfies.

1. **Open up the camera app.**
2. **Tap the selfie icon to switch to the front-facing camera.**
3. **Instead of PHOTO, choose PORTRAIT.**
4. **When you see a pleasant blur in the background, take the photo.**
5. **Go to your Photos app and compare the two photos.**

Figure 2-13 shows you an example of how the two different selfie camera modes present you to the world. It's usually the case that people like the PORTRAIT mode instead of the PHOTO mode for selfies, as the background blur makes the entire photo more pleasing to look at.

FIGURE 2-13:
A comparison of
the normal selfie
and the portrait
selfie.

The selfie camera has so many more wonderful features, and you can read about them to a greater level of detail in Chapter 4. Keep in mind that not all older model iPhones have Portrait mode.

Knowing When to Use (and not Use) the Camera Flash

With the advent of the iPhone 11 series models, you don't need to worry too much about when to use the flash. With intelligent software wizardry, Apple has been able to create flash-free, evenly lit photographs that were previously impossible. Apple believes in its technology so much that if you turn your flash to Auto mode, you may not even see it fire unless you're in a very dark environment.

You can easily access the flash by tapping on the little lightning bolt icon at the top left of your screen, as shown in Figure 2-14. Please keep in mind that the iPhone X and earlier series models look a bit different, but the functionality is pretty much the same.

Try the iPhone 11 series flash operation, visually illustrated in Figure 2-15:

FIGURE 2-14: The flash icon set to the On position for both the 11 series and also the X and earlier series iPhones.

1. Tap your flash icon at the top left to the On position.

2. Tap the arrow icon in the upper middle of your screen.

3. At the bottom left of your camera screen, tap the flash icon.

4. **Choose Flash Auto if you are unsure of when your photos will need a flash.**

   (Your iPhone will choose to activate the flash based on its assessment of the scene.)

5. **Choose On if you want to force the flash to fire for every shot you take, even if your photo may not really need the flash to fire.**

6. **Choose Off to return your flash to the never fire position, which is what most people use as a default for their photography.**

7. **To return to the normal camera's app appearance, tap the arrow at the top middle of your camera screen.**

FIGURE 2-15: Screenshot samples of iPhone 11 series flash operation.

If you have an iPhone X series or earlier model, flash operation is super simple:

1. **Tap the flash icon at the top left of your iPhone camera screen.**

2. **Choose either Auto, On, or Off using the same decision-making parameters that you just read about in the preceding iPhone 11 flash instructions.**

3. **Take your photo, remembering to switch back to flash off mode when finished.**

If you have your iPhone with you right now, please take two test photos of the exact same object, such as your coffee cup or a can of soda. The first one should be with the flash on, and the second one without the flash on. Upon reviewing your two test photos, which one do you like the best? Figure 2-16 gives you a typical result if you can't do your own test-run right now.

FIGURE 2-16:
A side-by-side comparison of flash on versus flash off.

Most of the time viewers prefer the photo without the flash. The primary reason for this choice is that a flash tends to flatten out the look of the object being photographed. What previously had a three-dimensional organic appearance, now has a cold-looking, two-dimensional feel. A flash usually takes viewers outside of what they're used to seeing with their own eyes, to a view that is far less appealing due to the harsh, artificial, and directional light source.

You may be wondering when you would ever even bother with the flash. The following list can help you make your decision:

Turn on Auto Flash when you are

» In a poorly lit room photographing a specific object that isn't too large

» Photographing receipts for business (take the photo at a slight angle for best results)

» Doing selfies in darker environments

» Taking fun snapshots of kids playing

» Photographing an object or person with light shining from behind them

» Unsure of when a photo would be better with a flash

Turn flash on when you are

» Documenting scientific or medical findings

>> Creating progress report photos of detailed work if you're a contractor

>> Doing any trade-related work that favors sharp detail over artistic appearance

Try not to use your flash for

>> Artistic and creative photos

>> Portraits of people (selfies are an exception)

>> Product photography

>> Any large space, as the flash won't be strong enough to illuminate the room

>> Pretty much any scenario where you want an attractive, natural looking image

"But what about all those amazing images from photographers who use flash all the time? Why do they get such great results?" This question is valid. The term *on-camera flash* refers to cameras of any type that have the flash built into the camera body (such as all smartphone cameras that have flashes). Figure 2-17 shows you what the flash looks like on the iPhone 11 Pro Max. Regardless of what model you have, the flashes on all iPhones are very close to the camera lens, which is not ideal for flattering light.

FIGURE 2-17:
The location of an iPhone flash.

An *off-camera* flash setup is what the amateurs and pros use for stunning flash photography. Their flash or flashes are not attached to their camera, and they have different ways to make sure that their flashes fire at the same time that they take their photo. Because their flash(es) are not illuminating the subject directly straightforward (as in your iPhone), the subject maintains its sense of *three-dimensionality* and organic look.

TIP

Keep in mind, though, that with advancements in electronics, optics, and programming, each generation of iPhone produces better and better flash photographs. A great example is the selfie camera's (front-facing camera) flash. While it's technically not a flash but a full screen of continuous light, it produces remarkably good facial illumination when photographing yourself or you with a friend.

Give it a try . . . switch your camera to selfie mode, turn your flash to the On position, and take the photo. If you have kept your iPhone updated (the most recent operating system), then you will see a pleasing warm light fill your entire screen. Figure 2-18 shows how the selfie camera shines with a warmish-looking soft light.

FIGURE 2-18:
The selfie camera's method for illuminating faces.

Getting to Know Live Photos

Live Photos first started as a bit of a gimmick a few years ago, but has been refined substantially to the point where they're a fantastic way to express yourself.

A *Live Photo* is a series of photos taken 1.5 seconds before and 1.5 seconds after you press the shutter release button. When your Live Photo capture is complete, the result is similar to a normal video. The quick video clip is fun to share with friends, as you can choose the very best-looking still photo from a choice of many still photos that make up the Live Photo. As it's a fun option and not really made for serious art photography, Live Photos are usually created between friends or of events with family members.

Chapter 15 offers a deeper dive into Live Photos. This section primarily helps you turning Live Photos on and off. Figure 2-19 displays the Live Photo icon for both the 11 series and the X series and earlier iPhone models.

FIGURE 2-19:
The Live Photo icons for the two current iOS versions.

Using Live Photo

When the icon has a diagonal line through it, Live Photo is turned off. If no line goes through the icon, Live Photo is activated. Follow these steps to create and view your first Live Photo:

1. **Find moving subjects, such as cars going by or trees swaying in the wind.**

   If you don't see any moving subjects, you can physically move your iPhone for a similar effect.

2. **Tap the circular Live Photo icon.**

3. **When ready, tap the normal shutter button to take the Live Photo.**

   Your Live Photo pops up in your Photos App, with a LIVE icon at the top left.

4. **Press and hold your finger anywhere within your photo.**

   Live Photo is activated, giving you about a three-second video clip.

To turn Live Photo off, simply tap the Live photo icon again.

Making sure Live Photo isn't on by default

If Live Photos is turned on by default, you're running the risk of using up more space on your iPhone and your iCloud storage quota. If you have a generous amount of internal and cloud storage space, having Live Photo on all the time won't be an issue. However, for those with 32GB or possibly 64GB iPhone models, it's usually best to keep Live Photo off and simply turn it on only when needed.

To turn off Live Photo by default, do the following:

1. **Turn off Live Photo at the top of your camera app screen.**
2. **In your iPhone Settings app, scroll down until you see Camera.**
3. **Within Camera, tap Preserve Settings.**

   Make sure that the Live Photo toggle is green, as in Figure 2-20.

   Live Photo will remember that you want it to be off from now on.

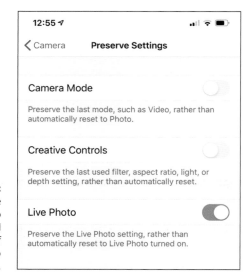

FIGURE 2-20:
Tap the Live Photo toggle to green to remind your camera of your Live Photo preferences.

Using the Camera Timer for Stable and Sharp Photos

Your iPhone has a count-down timer that allows for a delay between the time that you tap the shutter release button and the time that the photo is actually taken. This delay comes in two different time options: a three-second delay and a ten-second delay.

TIP

The three-second timer delay is popular for landscape and product photographers as it diminishes the chance of camera shake due to the photographer touching the iPhone.

The ten-second timer delay is useful for group family portraiture when you (as the photographer) need to set your iPhone up on a tripod and then run into the group so that you can be included in the photo.

To activate either timer, follow these instructions based on your model of iPhone:

>> **For iPhone 11 series models:** Tap on the top-middle arrow to reveal the extra options. Tap on the icon that looks like a clock timer and choose either 3s or 10s, as shown in Figure 2-21.

>> **For X series models and earlier:** Tap the timer icon at the top of your camera screen and choose either 3s or 10s. Tap the shutter button to take your photo and watch the countdown on your screen.

When the camera starts to take the photo, it will take ten consecutive photos rapidly. When you're doing group family photos, inevitably one person is blinking or making a funny face, which can ruin the entire photo unless you have decent photo-editing skills! To avoid this problem, you get to choose the best image out of ten images taken.

To choose the best of the ten photos, follow these easy steps:

1. **Go to your Photos app and locate the photo that you just took.**

2. **Tap Select at the bottom middle of your screen (see Figure 2-22).**

   This option is visible only if you see an icon at the top left of your screen that reads Burst (10 photos).

   At the very bottom of your screen, you have the option to scroll through ten photos that pretty much look identical (see Figure 2-23).

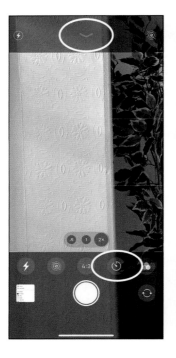

3. **Tap on the little circle icon at the bottom right of the photo that you like the best.**

   The icon now changes to blue and includes a check mark (see Figure 2-24).

4. **Tap Done at the top right.**

5. **To keep all the photos, tap the Keep Everything option; to keep just the single photo that you chose as the best, choose the Keep Only 1 Favorite option (see Figure 2-25).**

You don't need to choose only one best photo. Feel free to choose as many favorite photos as you like by tapping multiple circle icons at the bottom right of each photo that you'd like to keep.

Family portraits

To create successful family portraits that include you in them, follow these simple steps:

1. **Gather your group within an attractive setting and flattering light, such as early morning or evening.**

FIGURE 2-24:
A blue check
mark activates
when you tap on
your favorite of
the ten photos.

FIGURE 2-25:
To save space on
your device,
choose the Keep
Only 1 Favorite
option.

2. **Put your camera on a tripod or propped up on a stable surface, such as a fence or large boulder.**

3. **Ask the group to save a space for you when it's time to get into the composition.**

4. **Press the 10s option, and as soon as you see the numbers start to count down, quickly join the group.**

   If you see a little white light flashing every second next to your camera lens, everything is working normally.

   The flashes intensify, giving you about a two-second warning that the camera will take the photo.

When reviewing your group photo, you can choose the best family portrait then, or choose on another day. There is no time limit to choosing the best photo out of the ten taken.

Selfies with a tripod or stand

iPhones are adept at taking quality selfies. However, seeing such a large and close-up view of your face on the screen can sometimes feel a bit awkward. Maybe you feel that your face takes up a huge amount of the selfie photo!

To remedy this problem, you can back away a bit from the camera to allow more of the background and surroundings into your selfie. Choose a tripod, a mobile device stand set on a stable platform, or a selfie stick to allow your camera to be further from your face. (Check out Chapter 4 for more details on these accessories.)

With your iPhone on a tripod or a stand, choose the three-second timer. The three seconds give you enough time to take your hand away from the camera and establish your brilliant smile!

Landscape photography using your timer

Landscape photographers love using the three-second timer to create incredible tack-sharp photos. Did you know that even the act of tapping your camera's shutter button can cause the minutest amount of camera shake?

To avoid camera shake when your iPhone is on a tripod, set up your landscape scene as you like (more on Landscape photography in Chapter 5) and then take your photo using the three-second timer.

TIP

The three-second timer is better than the ten-second timer for landscapes because even within ten seconds, the lighting outside may change, ruining your brilliant landscape photo.

Either after your photo has been taken or in a warm café sipping your cappuccino, choose the best of ten landscape photos. Do they all look the same to you? If so, the iPhone has an incredible feature created just for you!

TIP

When you're reviewing your landscape photo in the Photos app and you press Select, do you see that your iPhone has already selected the photo that it thinks is best? It's signified by a little gray dot at the bottom of one of the ten photos just taken. iPhone thinks this photo is the sharpest, and you can accept its judgment or choose your own best photo.

TECHNICAL STUFF

You may be wondering how your iPhone could possibly know what photo is best. Well, it all comes down to advancements in Artificial Intelligence, and your iPhone's brilliant programming. The computer will analyze all ten photos almost instantly and choose the photo that exhibits the most amount of sharpness and other beneficial image qualities. Your iPhone is looking out for you!

Getting Creative with Filters

Your iPhone camera has ten creative filters that you can use for a quick and fun addition to your images. Accessing these filters is easy, and you can see in real time what the applied filter will look like even before you take the photo.

TIP

In the past, it was generally considered best practice to add a filter to your photo after the photo was taken rather than apply your filter before you tap the shutter button to take the photo.

That filter usage rule was extremely important advice before the advent of *nondestructive editing* (NDE), but now with NDE you can apply filters anytime you like. The term nondestructive editing means that within your Photos app, you can apply any filter either before or after you take the photo, and even years later, you can always revert back to the original unfiltered photo, with no loss of quality. Even when certain filters go out of style you can always go back to square-one.

Chapter 11 goes into filter usage to a greater level than what follows. To access the filters, follow these steps:

1. **Open your camera as if you were taking a normal photo.**

2. **On an iPhone 11, tap the top-middle arrow to access the camera extras, as in Figure 2-26.**

FIGURE 2-26:
The upper-middle arrow icon opens up your extra Camera app features.

3. **Tap on the last icon that resembles three overlapping circles, as shown in Figure 2-27.**

4. **Tap on Vivid, as in Figure 2-28.**

    You see a boost in color vibrancy.

    The next option is Vivid Warm and then seven more filter options.

5. **After cycling through all filters, choose your favorite and then take your photo.**

    Check out Figure 2-29, which shows what each filter effect does to a single scene in front of the iPhone.

Choosing the best camera filter for your photograph

While some of the supplied filters may seem to be a bit gimmicky, at times you will want to use a color photo simply for a sense of fun. For example, some of the filters that have the word Warm in their title are usually good for family photos and shots of your kids.

FIGURE 2-27:
Tap on the Filters icon that looks like three overlapping circles.

FIGURE 2-28:
When you tap Vivid or any other filter, you see an immediate change to your photo.

FIGURE 2-29:
Visual changes to
your photo based
on filter choice.

Filters with the word Cool in their title are often useful for artistic photographs that are helped by the filter's mood-altering capabilities.

Experiment with the three black-and-white filters to change almost any type of color photo into an artistic image that would be worthy to hang on your wall.

Reverting to the original

Don't like your filter choice? No problem! To revert to the original photo, all you need to do is

1. **Open your Photos app and locate your photo.**
2. **Tap the word Edit at the top right of your screen.**
3. **Tap on the word Revert written in red and then tap Revert to Original.**

    Your photo is now back to its normal nonfiltered state.

Feel free to repeat this process of filtering and reverting as much as you like. There are no limits to how many times you alter your photo within the Photos app, as you can always return to the original with no loss of quality.

Chapter **3**

Setting Up Your Camera for Photographic Greatness

I n this chapter, you discover all the ways to make your iPhone's photography workflow as seamless and as powerful as possible. In the same way that a custom shop can radically enhance the performance of a normal assembly line car, you can fully tune up your iPhone's camera with the tips in this chapter.

While this chapter isn't really about the physical act of taking a photo, it does set your camera up to take better photos by altering a few different Settings options.

Turning on iCloud Photos

As of this writing, everyone who buys and registers an iPhone using iCloud automatically receives 5GB of free cloud storage. If you're not familiar with iCloud or even what cloud storage is, here's how it works:

1. **You take a photo on your iPhone.**

2. **When on Wi-Fi, that photo is automatically sent to the Apple computer servers.**

3. **Your photo now lives in the cloud, which simply means a large data storage facility.**

4. **When you need to have your full-resolution photo, it will download back to your iPhone.**

So why bother with the complexity of your photo going up to the cloud and then back down? There are a number of reasons why this process is helpful, but the one that is usually the most valued is based on theft, damage, and loss of your iPhone. If you have an unfortunate iPhone problem and you can't access your data anymore, no worries. All your photos and iPhone data are stored safely on the cloud!

Before setting up iCloud so that your photos are safe, you may rightfully ask how secure and safe iCloud is and whether it protects your valuable digital assets. While no cloud backup is 100 percent safe against natural or purposeful damage, Apple has a very good data privacy track record compared to the international average of other company's cloud security reputation. Still, you can always skip this step if you're not convinced, and you can create just as great photos.

To set up iCloud to automatically send your photos to the cloud, follow these steps:

1. **Open the Settings app.**

2. **Scroll down until you see the option of tapping Photos.**

3. **When inside the Photos settings page, tap the iCloud Photos toggle on so that it turns green (see Figure 3-1).**

On the off-chance that you can't access some of the preceding steps, you may be signed out of your Apple ID. Tap on your name at the top of the Settings page and scroll to the bottom of the Apple ID page. If you don't see the words Sign Out in red, you need to sign in to access iCloud (see Figure 3-2).

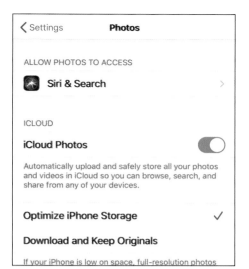

FIGURE 3-1:
Toggle iCloud
Photos on.

FIGURE 3-2:
If you see the
words Sign Out,
you're signed in
to your Apple ID.

Optimizing iPhone Storage

Your iPhone has a really intelligent way to allow you to take far more photos than what you could normally store on your mobile device. If you chose to turn on iCloud Photos, you can save a massive amount of internal storage space on your iPhone. When your photos upload to the cloud, there will be a smaller resolution and lesser quality photo stored in your phone, and the large original master version of the photo will be stored in iCloud.

The nice thing about this arrangement is that you can edit your lower res versions as if they were the original master versions. Your editing instructions go up to the cloud, and the cloud versions get edited exactly the way you want them edited.

Figure 3-3 shows Optimize iPhone Storage checked, which means that the large resolution master photos will always go up to iCloud and your editable smaller versions will stay in your iPhone. This is the ultimate tool to free up valuable space on your device.

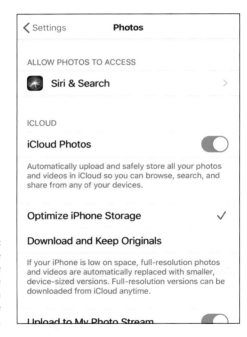

FIGURE 3-3: Turn Optimize iPhone Storage on if you're running low on iPhone storage space.

If you have an iPhone with 64GB of storage or less, you may want to consider turning on this feature so that you have space for other things like apps, podcasts, music, or anything else.

If you have an iPhone with 128GB of storage or more and your photo collection is not all that large, you may be able to get away with keeping this option off. That will mean that your originals are still saved in the cloud, but the versions on the phone are of the same original master quality. This option is perfectly fine, but keep in mind that as your photo collection grows, you may find yourself running out of iPhone storage space. If and when this happens, you'll probably want to toggle this option on.

To find out how much storage space your iPhone model has, follow these steps.

1. **In Settings, scroll down to locate General and tap on it.**

2. **Locate and tap on the words iPhone Storage.**

   At the top of the page, you see how many gigabytes you've used and how many are remaining (see Figure 3-4).

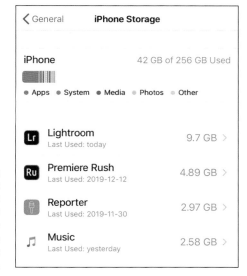

FIGURE 3-4:
The iPhone Storage section shows you how much iPhone storage space you have remaining.

If your phone is low on storage, make sure to optimize your iPhone storage.

Downloading the Original Photos

After setting up your iPhone to send all photos into the cloud for ultimate optimization, you would be tempted to ask why would anyone feel the need to go back to having all of those large photos on their iPhones.

One reason is that if iPhone users upgrade from an older model iPhone to one with a large storage capacity, such as a 32GB model to a 256GB model, they can afford the space that their original master photos would take up within their new iPhone storage.

Another reason that some people tap the Download and Keep Originals is for when they want to export a lot of photos to external hard drives. It's much easier to let your iPhone download the master photos overnight while you're sleeping, so that you have access to a quicker transfer the next day. Keep in mind that if you choose this option, your iPhone storage will probably fill up quickly, depending on how many photos and videos you've taken over the years.

Regardless of your reasons, the option is always there to return your photos back to full storage on your device, as shown in Figure 3-5. Keep in mind that your photos are still safely copied in the cloud, even if you stop doing photo optimization.

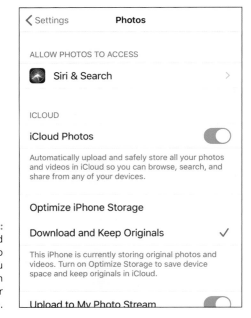

FIGURE 3-5:
Tap Download and Keep Originals if you have enough space on your iPhone.

Uploading to My Photo Stream

My Photo Stream is a service that allows you to freely store up to 30 days or 1,000 photos in the cloud, even if you don't pay for iCloud storage. My Photo Stream was a really great way to sync photos to your various devices prior to Apple's iCloud

Photo Library service. However, these days most people keep this option turned off by default.

Keep in mind this easy decision-making parameter when deciding to use My Photo Stream:

» If you don't want to upgrade from the free 5GB iCloud storage tier but you have more than 5GB of photos, it may be beneficial to turn on My Photo Stream.

» For all other users, keep My Photo Stream turned off, as shown in Figure 3-6, as it's really not necessary. Your iCloud Photo Library's automatic cloud uploading will take good care of you!

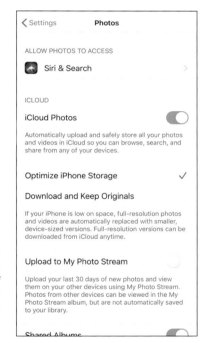

FIGURE 3-6:
Keep My Photo Stream turned off if you plan to take a lot of photos and use iCloud Photo Library.

Sharing Albums

Did your dog just perform the best trick ever? Did your grandchild create a funny face that begs to be shared with the rest of the family? You probably have countless reasons to share photo albums with friends and family, and your iPhone's Photos app allows you to do just that.

First of all, take a look at the toggle shown in Figure 3-7 within the Photos settings page. There is really no reason to have this toggle turned off. Even if you actually never get around to sharing photo albums with friends, it doesn't hurt to just keep this toggle in the green *on* position.

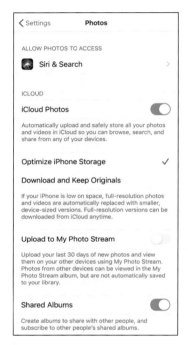

FIGURE 3-7:
Keep the Shared Albums toggle to the on position by default, even if you don't yet share photos.

This section tells you how to turn on the Shared Albums feature, not how to actually use the feature. If you want to share photo albums, take a look at Chapter 13.

Watching Cellular Data

You've probably heard horror stories of smartphone users going over their data quota and owing their mobile provider hundreds of dollars in data overage fees. While a lot of companies now give warnings when you're nearing the data limit for your particular monthly phone plan, it's still wise to watch your Photos data consumption. You can do so by following a few simple steps:

1. **In your Photos settings page, tap on the words Cellular Data.**

2. **Toggle the Cellular Data option off or on (see Figure 3-8).**

If you have a limited mobile data plan, toggle the Cellular Data option to the off position. Data transfers will happen only over Wi-Fi.

If you have a generous data plan, you may want to toggle Cellular Data on, but keep Unlimited Updates off. Your iPhone will restrict data transfers to a reasonable amount per day to avoid data overages.

If you have an unlimited data plan with your mobile provider, you could keep both options toggled green, which keeps your photos updated all the time without the need for Wi-Fi.

FIGURE 3-8:
Minimal mobile data usage without Wi-Fi, chosen by tapping Cellular Data to the on position, for those with large mobile data plans.

WARNING

There is a danger in having both of these cell data options turned on. Say that you have an unlimited data plan and choose to have both Cellular Data and Unlimited Updates turned on. But then later on, you downgrade your mobile data plan and forget to turn these toggles off. You run the risk of going over your data plan quickly, depending on how frequently you take photos. If you're in doubt, turn both off, which restricts all photos-related data to Wi-Fi connections only.

Auto-Playing Videos and Live Photos

Within your Photos settings page, the next option is called Auto-Play Videos and Live Photos, located just under the words PHOTOS TAB. When this toggle is set to the green-colored on position, your videos and Live Photos will start playing automatically when you preview your video within the Photos app.

When the Auto-Play option is turned off, you will need to press the play icon in the center of the video to watch it, as the video won't start playing by itself.

So, which one do you choose? It doesn't really matter one way or the other, as it's mostly personal preference. One could possibly argue that having Auto-Play turned off would save battery power, but it would probably be so minimal that you wouldn't even notice.

Viewing Full HDR

HDR stands for *High Dynamic Range,* which is a process where your iPhone takes three photos of the same scene, but at three different exposures. One exposure is bright, the other normal, and the third photo is dark. The camera then does some mixing of these three photos to give you a final photo that has the best tonal qualities of all three photos, mixed into one very well-exposed photo.

With the option of View Full HDR turned on, you can see the effects of your HDR photo in real-time. Why not keep this option turned on? It's always nice to see what your photo looks like just after you take it.

Transferring to Mac or PC

The last option on your Photos settings page is labeled as TRANSFER TO MAC OR PC. This option allows for the transfer of what are called *High Efficiency* image and video files to either be converted to universally readable formats, such as the well-known JPEG format. As this option is a bit technical and involves new files formats called HEIC and HEVC, here is an easy decision-making parameter:

>> Are you a beginner or hobbyist iPhone photographer? If yes, choose Automatic.

>> Are you an advanced amateur who is adept at photo and video editing? If so, choose Keep Originals.

If you're in doubt as to which of the two options best describes your level of photo and video editing, it's probably best to choose Automatic, which will guarantee a smooth transition from your iPhone to some Windows computers or many older devices.

Customizing Your iPhone's Camera

The extremely useful Camera option takes you out of the Photos app setting page and into your Camera's settings page. Go back to your iPhone's Settings app and then scroll down and tap on the Camera icon, which looks like Figure 3-9.

As soon as you have your Camera settings page open, you see options similar to Figure 3-10. If you have an X series model iPhone or earlier, your options may be slightly different.

>> **Preserve Settings:** If you want your iPhone to remember to activate your last mode, such as switching to video because your last capture was video, then turn on Camera Mode. If you like to use the same filter or other creative control on your next photo automatically, turn on Creative Controls.

   Usually these two options are left off, as most photographers tend to want to start fresh with each new photo opportunity. However, if you're doing a photo shoot for a client and they always want the same filtered look for each capture, then you may want to choose to engage these Preserved Settings options.

   The Live Photo option is best left to the on position, however. This setting allows you to selectively activate Live Photo instead of it always being on, which may be handy for users who don't have much storage space left on their iPhones.

>> **Grid:** Turn the grid on for architectural and landscape photos or to study the Rule of Thirds (see Chapter 5). Turn the grid off if you find it distracting.

>> **Scan QR codes:** Turn this option on to retrieve shopping and product information by photographing the code supplied by a retailer. Your camera then opens the retailer's website in your Safari mobile browser.

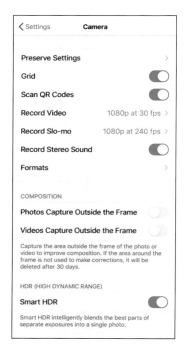

FIGURE 3-10:
Your Camera
settings page.

>> **Record Video:** Unless you have video creation and editing experience and can make good use of 4k, at this point 1080p HD at 30 fps is fine for your normal video of kids and family events. If you're running low on space on your iPhone, choose 720p HD at 30 fps. If you also see the option to choose Auto Low Light FPS, turn it on. You can find out more about video creation in Chapter 14.

>> **Record Slo-Mo:** Choose 1080p HD at 240 fps for really cool looking slow-motion effects. If you're concerned about running out of space on your iPhone, choose 1080 HD at 120 fps.

>> **Record Stereo Sound:** Turn Record Stereo Sound to the on position, which gives your viewers a better audio experience.

>> **Formats:** Choose High Efficiency, which reduces the file size of your photos and videos. These file formats are new, so not all devices understand them yet, but your iPhone has you covered. You can choose Automatic to be assured that you can share your photos and videos to devices that can't yet read High Efficiency file formats. (See the section "Transferring to Mac or PC," earlier in this chapter.

WARNING

Choose Most Compatible only if you have a technical or industry-specific reason for doing so. These JPEG and H.264 files are internationally readable; however, they take up about double the amount of space on your iPhone.

>> **Composition:** If your iPhone has these options, turn them on for greater cropping abilities, which I discuss in greater detail in Chapter 11. Turn these options off if you like the challenge of photographing exactly what you see, wanting no extra help with composition choices.

>> **Smart HDR:** Turn Smart HDR on as a default setting, as it will do a great job of giving you an evenly exposed photo. If you're an advanced iPhone photographer who prefers to do HDR photos by yourself in Adobe Photoshop or other software, turn this option off. If you are an avid street photographer who likes gritty images with plenty of deep shadows, turn Smart HDR off. Just remember to turn it back on again when photographing lighter-toned subjects, such as family, nature, and landscapes.

Chapter **4**

Applying iPhone Auto-Mode Settings

In this chapter, you go beyond taking normal photos to creating advanced selfie photos. I also cover square and panoramic photos so that you know exactly why you should use these options and when to choose them to serve your creative vision.

Zooming with Various Camera Modes

Zooming in to your subject can visually bring distant objects closer so that they fill your iPhone camera's screen. However, the ability to zoom in or out works with only some photography modes. If you have your iPhone with you, you can follow along with these camera modes and their zooming abilities:

» **Selfie photos:** No zooming is available for iPhone X series models or earlier. A slightly wider zoom is available for iPhone 11 series models, which I explain in the section "Taking Selfies," later in this chapter.

» **Square photos:** All optical and digital zooming functionality is available in the same way that zooming works on normal photos.

>> **Portrait photos:** No zooming is available when using your front-facing selfie camera. However, your rear-facing camera allows for optical zoom if you have a multilens iPhone.

>> **Panoramics:** Digital zoom is not available, but optical zoom is based on how many lenses your iPhone has.

Preparing to Take Selfies

When you have your Camera app open, you can flip the lens view from what is called the *rear-facing view* to the *front-facing view*. A selfie photo makes use of the *front-facing* camera lens.

You can take selfies within a number of camera modes, such as square photos, videos, portraits, time-lapses, and slo-mo videos. In the following sections, you discover the best ways to use the selfie camera within the mode called Portrait, which allows for a lovely background blur behind your head. (For details on how to access the selfie camera, check out Chapter 2.)

Lighting and background

To create a great selfie, follow these best practices:

>> Look for a background like Figure 4-1 that is intriguing and will present you well, but one that is not so radical that it competes with your face for attention.

>> Make sure that the light is not solely coming from behind you, as your face will be in shadow.

>> Overcast days or being in a shadowy area will produce the softest looking selfies.

>> Being in direct sunlight is harsher light and may not look too appealing.

>> Being illuminated by soft morning or evening light is very attractive.

>> If you're doing a selfie indoors, try to angle yourself so that your face is illuminated by a large window, as in Figure 4-2 and Figure 4-3.

>> If no window is available, try not to stand directly under a ceiling light, which will cause harsh shadows under your eyebrows and nose.

FIGURE 4-1:
Choose a
background that
looks appealing
but doesn't pull
attention away
from your face.

FIGURE 4-2:
Face a large
window for
indoor selfies.

FIGURE 4-3:
Using large
window light your
face will be evenly
illuminated.

Light case options

TIP

Illuminated iPhone protective cases are effective for adding even-looking light when you're creating selfies at night. An illuminated iPhone light case plus your selfie flash will give you plenty of photo opportunities, even in very dark environments.

Check out Figure 4-4, which shows two Tokyo women photographing themselves with an illuminated smartphone case.

At the time of this writing, the company Lumee produces some really great illuminated iPhone case options. They have cases that illuminate only your face, and some that have lights on both sides of the case, which means they will perform double duty as a way to also illuminate rear-facing objects that you want to photograph normally.

Selfie sticks and stabilizers

One of the greatest complaints about selfie-taking is that people are self-conscious about how they look when they take the photo. One major factor for this criticism is that their face is often disproportionately large within the composition. To help with this problem, use a selfie stick or a smartphone stabilizer to extend your iPhone farther away from your face.

FIGURE 4-4:
An illuminated
smartphone
protective case
that helps with
nighttime selfies.

TIP

When your iPhone is really close to your face, a certain amount of unattractive distortion naturally happens. When you extend your iPhone away from your face a little bit, your face has a more natural looking appearance.

Selfie sticks

Selfie sticks are cheap and easy to use, and you can often find them at department stores or any type of store that sells electronics. They look like wands, and you can extend their distance by twisting the stick to various lengths.

REMEMBER

Selfie sticks are wonderful because they're small and lightweight, and you can take them anywhere. The only downside is that you need to keep your grip on them steady, as even the smallest level of wind can make your arm a bit unsteady when you're just about to take the photo.

TIP

Selfie sticks often have a trigger at the base of the stick that will act as a remote shutter release. This trigger is helpful as you won't need to reach all the way to your iPhone to tap the shutter button. Each selfie stick usually comes with instructions on how to set up the remote release for easy selfie taking.

If your selfie stick doesn't have a remote shutter release, no problem. Simply activate your three- or 10-second timer, reposition your selfie stick so that you look good in the frame, and then be ready for your photo when the timer has counted down and has taken the photo. (To find out how to access the self-timers, take a look at Chapter 2.)

Stabilizers

Technically called a *gimble,* this selfie solution is battery-powered and extremely good at giving you a stable apparatus for selfies, even if you don't have steady hands or if there is a breeze outside.

The gimble senses any movement while you're ready to take your photo, and it counteracts that movement near instantly to maintain a steady hold on your iPhone. These gimble stabilizers are a real boon for social media influencers, film-makers, and iPhone photographers.

The gimble stabilizer is an excellent choice for near-flawless selfies. Keep in mind that they're usually pricy, larger than selfie sticks, need battery power, and not as easy to pack around with you. However, the benefits highly outweigh those drawbacks.

The Osmo Mobile 3 is a fantastic gimble to choose if you're in the market for a battery-powered stabilizer. Figure 4-5 shows you an example of the Osmo folded for storage, and Figure 4-6 shows the Osmo powered-up and ready to roll.

FIGURE 4-5:
The Osmo Mobile 3 gimble stabilizer folded up for packing.

FIGURE 4-6:
The Osmo
powered up
ready to take a
selfie photo.

Taking Selfies

With your background chosen and the light appealing, you're ready to create your selfie. To do so, you need to complete the following steps, which are described in detail in later sections:

1. **Choose the Portrait selfie mode.**

2. **Adjust the depth control.**

3. **Choose your favorite type of selfie light.**

4. **Fine-tune the light intensity.**

5. **Add photo filters.**

6. **Add a flash.**

7. **Use a self-timer.**

8. **(Optional) Adjust the selfie zoom to include your friends in the photo.**

Choose the Portrait selfie mode

To take a selfie, you need to switch to the selfie lens so that you can see yourself. To do so, tap on PORTRAIT. Keep the flash at the top left off for now.

Do you see a soft blurry background? If so, you're in Portrait mode, as shown in Figure 4-7.

FIGURE 4-7: Portrait mode creates a soft background blur behind your head for pleasing portraits.

Adjust depth control

Depth control is a clever way to adjust how much background blur you'd like in your selfies. Maybe you want a lot of background blur to mimic the look of a professional DSLR lens, or maybe you want less background blur to make out a bit of detail in the background. To access depth control, follow these steps:

1. **Tap on the little *f* icon at the top right of your screen while still in Portrait mode.**

   Underneath your photo is a sliding *f-scale*, which affects how much soft blur you see behind you.

2. **Scroll left and right and choose the amount of blur that you feel looks the best.**

   The lower f-numbers produce more background blur, and the higher f-numbers remove background blur. F4.5 is usually a default amount of blur that looks great for most selfies, as illustrated in Figure 4-8.

   Figure 4-9 shows what enhanced background blur looks like at the extreme ends of f1.4. Figure 4-10 is an example of the maximum amount of depth-of-field focus sharpness of f16, where there is little to no background blur.

FIGURE 4-8:
The default f4.5 gives you a moderate and pleasing amount of background blur.

FIGURE 4-9:
f1.4 produces a lot of background blur.

Tap the f icon at the top right of your screen again to return to the normal camera view.

Choose your favorite type of selfie light

In addition to the default NATURAL LIGHT option, as shown in Figure 4-11, you have many light choices for your selfie:

» **STUDIO LIGHT:** Softens skin and mimics professional photo studio lighting (see Figure 4-12).

» **CONTOUR LIGHT:** Adds definition and shadow to your face while still maintaining smooth skin. This option provides slightly more dramatic selfies, as the side of your face appears to have a more sculpted, shadow area similar to fashion-oriented photo studio lighting (see Figure 4-13).

» **STAGE LIGHT:** Creates black backgrounds (see Figure 4-14).

» **STAGE LIGHT MONO:** Creates a moody, dark bio-pic selfie that commands attention (see Figure 4-15).

FIGURE 4-11:
Natural Light is
the default look
for your Portrait
mode selfies.

FIGURE 4-12:
The Studio Light
option is great for
skin smoothening
and replicating a
photo studio
environment.

FIGURE 4-14:
Stage Light creates an artificial black background replicating photo studios with black background studio paper.

>> **HIGH-KEY LIGHT MONO:** The opposite of the previous STAGE LIGHT MONO, gives you a black-and-white photo bathed in a beautiful wash of white light (see Figure 4-16).

What do you think? Pretty impressive isn't it? You now have so many combina-tions to create the perfect selfie depending on your mood and your location.

Fine-tune the light intensity and your effect intensity

In addition to customizing lighting, you can customize the amount of the effect. In other words, you can adjust the intensity of each look on a percentage scale from 0 to 100. This is very useful if you feel that the intensity of, for example, Stage Light, is too over the top. Simply reduce the intensity of Stage Light (or any other type of light) to the point that you like the effect results.

>> Tap on the hexagon icon at the top right of your screen, which is next to the f icon. A sliding scale appears at the bottom of your photo, and it usually defaults at a level of 50, as shown in Figure 4-17.

FIGURE 4-16:
High-Key Light
Mono offers
a black-and-
white portrait
with a white
background.

FIGURE 4-17:
The default effect
intensity
is usually set at
50 percent, and
the scale is
adjustable.

Scroll left and right until you see the amount of white light that you like. The lower numbers have less light surrounding your selfie, such as in Figure 4-18, and the higher numbers have more light around you, which provides for a type of angelic looking glow, similar to Figure 4-19.

>> The scrolling filter level adjuster is available on all the options, such as Stage Light, Contour Light, and Studio Light. The only option where it's not available is NATURAL LIGHT because the Natural Light option doesn't add any light effects.

TIP

The scrolling levels adjustment also controls how much of a filter's effect is placed over your face. For example, on STUDIO LIGHT and the other light options, the most amount of skin smoothening happens at 100, where a level of 0 has little or no skin smoothening.

Take a look at Figure 4-20, which shows a default 50 percent skin smoothening within the Studio Light effect.

FIGURE 4-19: The most amount of lighting effect is visible at 100, which produces an angelic glow in this photo.

FIGURE 4-20: The skin smoothening benefits of *Studio Light* set at the default level of 50 percent.

The skin smoothening effect is not really necessary for young people who naturally have smooth skin, but it works really well for photos of the middle-aged author. Check out Figure 4-21, which shows a side-by-side comparison of the Studio Light skin smoothening effect set to 0 percent and then next to it, 100 percent. With a simple scroll of the intensity slider, you can see what is possible with such extreme effect adjustments.

FIGURE 4-21: A comparison of the Studio Light skin smoothening effects from 0 on the left to 100 percent on the right.

Add photo filters

You can also add photo filters to your selfies. At the top right of your camera screen, tap the hexagon icon to exit the light intensity options. The icon should have switched from yellow to white.

To access the built-in photo filters:

1. **Tap on NATURAL LIGHT.**

2. **Just below and slightly to the right of the NATURAL LIGHT icon, tap the filter icon that looks like three interconnecting circles.**

TIP

   If you don't see this icon, on an iPhone 11 model tap on the top middle arrow to reveal your camera's extra options, including the filter's interconnecting circle icon. If you have an X series model iPhone or earlier, tap on the filter's interconnecting circle icon at the top of your camera's screen.

3. **When you see the word ORIGINAL, tap each filter that is to the right of the previous filter.**

4. **Choose the filter that you feel makes you look the best.**

   Maybe none of them do! If so, switch back to ORIGINAL.

5. **To lock in your chosen filter or to maintain ORIGINAL with no filter applied, tap the filter's three interconnected circles icon to the immediate left of your filter options.**

Did you notice that each filter gets applied to your selfie while still maintaining the background blur? Figure 4-22 shows an example of the VIVID WARM filter applied, and the background blur is maintained. This great feature allows for a huge amount of choice when showing yourself to the world or maybe to just your best friend.

Add a flash

The next selfie option is to activate your flash, which you can find at the top left of your screen. (See Chapter 2 to get an in-depth look at the various flash functions that can help you with your photography.)

If you activate the selfie flash, you will be bathed in a soft warm light that comes from the entire iPhone screen. You can activate the flash during any of the depth and lighting modes.

Use your self-timer

It's often helpful to use your three-second self-timer for selfies, as those extra seconds allow you to compose yourself and get that brilliant smile ready.

On the iPhone 11 series models, you may need to tap the top middle arrow to return to the camera options. You then see the timer icon at the bottom next to the flash icon.

If you're using an iPhone X series model or earlier, your timer icon is at the top of your camera screen.

Go to Chapter 2 for an explanation of how to access and operate the three- or ten-second timer.

Adjust selfie zoom to add your friends into the picture

You can also take selfies with a friend, thanks to the iPhone 11 series models' wider zoom option.

To access and activate the wider zoom, follow these steps:

1. **Choose the normal PHOTO camera.**

2. **Activate the selfie camera mode by tapping the selfie front-facing icon at the bottom.**

3. **Place yourself and your friend into the frame, similar to Figure 4-23.**

FIGURE 4-23:
The normal selfie camera view including two people.

4. **Tap the diagonal icon that looks like two arrows pointing away from each other.**

   A wider selfie camera that can hopefully include you and your friends comfortably appears, as shown in Figure 4-24.

   You can either continue with this wider view or switch back to the tighter selfie view if you so desire.

FIGURE 4-24:
The wider zoomed out view is activated when you tap the dual-arrows icon.

Considering Square Photos

The social media and photo-sharing app Instagram was a huge influence on the popularity of square photos when the app was introduced to the world in 2010. Square photos are everywhere, but it's a good idea to know why you would choose a square photo, and when it's most effective.

While Instagram has allowed nonsquare photos to be uploaded for a number of years now, the public still really likes square uploads, which is what they're used to seeing when viewing Instagram photos. As the app was originally created solely for square images, it's designed to make square photos look good both in the preview area where you see all your Instagram photos and, of course, when you view a photo full size after tapping on its smaller thumbnail version.

TIP

You may want to have your grid lines activated for creating square photos (see Chapter 3). There are also times when you may want to have your grid lines activated for selfies, such as when you're positioning yourself in front of architecture or any natural or built-environment that has strong horizontal and/or vertical lines. The grid lines can help you compose the scene much better than not having them visible.

TIP

Figure 4-25 show you what is called the thumbnail grid view when you first access a person's Instagram profile. As the photos are all presented in the square format, many photographers have decided over the years to upload in the square format. This decision is not too critical these days as Instagram also accepts nonsquare photos.

Facebook also works well in square format. There is a lot of research done about the benefits of using square image formats compared to normal horizontal formats if you do any amount of Facebook advertising.

FIGURE 4-25:
The typical appearance of an Instagram profile showing square thumbnail photos.

FRAMING YOUR PHOTOS

Trying to figure out how to frame photos for your wall or to give your framed photos as gifts can be difficult. There are so many framing and matting size options, and often you won't know what looks good on the wall until you actually buy the frame and hang it.

If you consider presenting your framed work in a square format you will have an easier time of choosing frames and mattes, and potentially an easier time grouping photos together in a series to fill an empty space on a wall.

Accessing your square camera

The Square camera is easy to find on iPhone X series models and earlier:

1. **Open your camera app.**

   By default, the PHOTO option is usually activated.

2. **Scroll to the right and tap on SQUARE.**

3. **Take your first square photo.**

For the 11 series iPhone models, follow these steps:

1. **Open your Camera app.**

2. **In the top middle of your screen, tap the arrow that is pointing up so that it now points down.**

3. **Just above the circular shutter button, tap on the icon named 4:3.**

4. **Tap Square, which is to the immediate left of the 4:3 ratio.**

5. **Take your square photo choosing any lens or digital zoom that you like.**

   TIP

   You can even choose a square selfie photo if you want, by tapping the selfie icon at the bottom right.

Following square photography best practices

The square photography workflow has its advantages and disadvantages. Table 4-1 offers a quick summary to help you decide whether you should take your photograph in the square format or simply crop to a square after you take the photo.

TABLE 4-1   **Pros and Cons of Taking a Photo in a Square Format**

Pros	Cons
Quick and easy, with no cropping required	Less options for repurposing the photo for horizontal or vertical usage
Can upload to square-friendly social media sites as soon as you take the photo	Reduces the number of pixels in the overall photo, resulting in a lower resolution image file

TIP

If you have the time, it's better to take all photos in the normal camera's 4:3 ratio and simply crop to a square format after you take the photo. By cropping within your Photos app, you can always revert back to the original nonsquare photo for future photo repurposing.

Creating Panoramic Photos

A *panoramic photo* is a long photo that is not very high in relation to its length (see Figure 4-26).

FIGURE 4-26: Panoramic photos are longer than a standard horizontal photo.

Your iPhone allows you to create *panos* (short for panoramics) by capturing the very wide scene in front of your camera. As you slowly pan your camera from left to right, your iPhone is recording everything that it sees and then produces a very long final image. Think of a panoramic photo as many horizontal photos stitched together to form one long photo.

The value of creating panos is simply for the sake of good art. Do you love landscape photography and also enjoy seeing your work framed and hanging on a wall? If so, why not try creating a panoramic landscape and then framing that gem with a custom panoramic frame and a signed matte? It will look fantastic hanging on your wall.

Panoramic best practices for frame-worthy photographs

Panos require you to move your iPhone camera slowly and steadily and also in a relative straight line horizontally. The usual path is from the far left of your scene to the far right. Here are some steps that you can take to create your first pano masterpiece:

1. **Tap PANO, which is located to the far right of your camera modes, next to PORTRAIT.**

2. **Compose your photo so that you're starting your pano at the far left of whatever scene you're photographing (see Figure 4-27).**

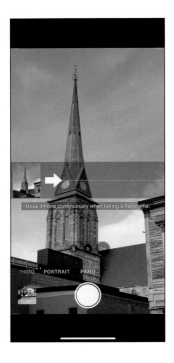

FIGURE 4-27:
The starting point of a left-to-right panoramic photo.

3. **Before you press the white shutter release button to take your pano, visually scan the far right side of your scene to estimate where you'll want to end your pano.**

4. **Press the shutter button and slowly move your iPhone from the far left to the far right.**

TIP

Try to keep the white arrow as close to the yellow horizontal line as possible. See Figure 4-28 for an example of left-to-right panning.

5. **When your screen has reached your predetermined end-point (the place where you want your pano to stop), simple press your shutter button to stop the panoramic.**

FIGURE 4-28:
Screenshots
showing the slow
left-to-right
horizontal iPhone
movement
needed to create
a pano.

And there you go! It's as simple as that to create frame–worthy wall art. Use panos for street scenes without people walking, cityscapes, and landscapes.

If you run into any problems simply try the pano again. And keep in mind that if a lot of moving vehicles or people are in your scene, you may get some strange results. If you can create your pano at a time when there isn't much movement in the general area, you will get the best–looking final image.

TIP

If you have a multilens iPhone, you can use your various lenses to produce your panoramics. On the 11 Pro models, you can choose between your three lens views, the ultra wide, wide, and telephoto lenses. On the dual lens models, you can choose to create your panos using your ultra wide or your wide angle lenses if you have an iPhone 11, or your wide and telephoto lenses if you own the X series or earlier dual lens iPhone models.

Vertical panoramic photos!

Very few people know about vertical panos, but they can be really fun. Try vertical panoramics in special nature environments, such as in Figure 4-29.

To take a vertical pano, rotate your iPhone so that it's horizontal instead of vertical and then follow the same steps as in the previous normal pano instructions. The only difference is that you'll be moving your iPhone camera from low to high, instead of from left to right.

FIGURE 4-29:
A vertical
panoramic
photographed in
a beautiful
Eastern European
forest.

2

Discovering the Fundamentals of Photographic Genres

Chapter **5**

Creating Perfect Landscape Photographs

O ne of the most popular photographic genres is landscape photography. These stunning scenic images help your viewer imagine themselves at the precipice of the Grand Canyon, the camel-trodden sand dunes of the Middle East, or the lush rain forests of the Amazon basin.

The reason that we find landscape photography endearing is because of our desire for adventure, for beauty, and for peace within our world. What lofty qualities! The landscape photo has a lot to live up to, and you can be a part of this rich history without even needing to leave your own region.

So, this chapter is all about you and how to jump-start you into iPhone landscape excellence. In this chapter, you discover both technical and artistic tips, tricks, and techniques to move you from snapshot shooter to landscape artist.

Note: Even if you don't care about landscape photography or can't do landscape photography because of mobility issues, please read through this chapter anyway. This chapter contains so many great tips and techniques that apply to almost all the photography genres that you'll encounter as an iPhone photographer.

Camera Considerations

Have you ever wondered why it's not critical that you manually focus your iPhone's lens? If you've ever used a film SLR camera, a DSLR, or a mirrorless digital camera, you already know that if you don't focus your lens either manually or automatically, your photo will be ruined.

TECHNICAL STUFF

iPhones and all other mobile device cameras (Android smartphones, iPads, tablets) have minimal focusing needs because of a number of technical factors. Smaller electronic sensors within mobile cameras allow for what is called *deep depth of field*. In simple terms, deep depth of field means that most everything in your ultra wide and wide angle iPhone composition will have sharp focus without the need for precise focusing at the level of a DSLR style camera and lens combination.

Take a look at Figure 5-1, which is an example of deep depth of field. The woman's face has focus sharpness, and so does the distant Matsumoto Castle in Japan.

FIGURE 5-1:
Deep depth of field means that both near and far subjects will have focus sharpness.

The larger the sensor size in your camera, the less amount of deep depth of field you will have. For example, a professional Canon or Nikon DSLR has the potential for *shallow depth of field*, which is actually very good for portraiture. The person's face will be sharp, but the foreground and background will be blurry.

Take a look at Figure 5-2, which is an example of shallow depth of field. The woman's face, of course, has focus sharpness, but the Japanese castle has a pleasant background blur.

FIGURE 5-2:
Shallow depth of field means that whatever is behind your properly focused subject will have a nice blurred look.

REMEMBER

While there are always exceptions to every rule, generally speaking, landscape photographers prefer a deep depth of field so that everything in their photo has focus sharpness. They tend to use wide lenses instead of telephoto lenses. In the world of iPhone photography, that means using your ultra wide and/or wide angle lenses.

Long-pressing the screen where your main subject is located

TIP

Most of the time, very little focusing is going on inside your iPhone's widest camera lenses. Sometimes, however, you might want to force the focus of your iPhone lens to make sure that a certain part of your landscape composition is guaranteed to be focused sharply.

Focusing errors rarely happen with iPhone's ultra wide and wide angle lenses; however, the telephoto lens that comes with many iPhone models may have focusing needs that require some of your input.

Take a look at Figure 5-3, which is a landscape that involves a foreground (the potted plant), a middle-ground (the trees), and a background (the hot-air balloon). As this photo was taken with an iPhone telephoto lens, there is a greater chance of having a focus error compared to a similar landscape shot using a wide or ultra wide iPhone lens.

FIGURE 5-3: When photographing landscapes with an iPhone telephoto lens, there may be foreground sections that are not focused sharply.

The potted plant is actually slightly out of focus, visible as a close-up in Figure 5-4. Everything in the background is tack-sharp, which is great, but the photograph could have been even better if I focused on the plant instead of just taking the photo with no manual focus intervention.

TIP

The slightly out-of-focus foreground potted plant issue of Figures 5-3 and 5-4 is due to the fact that telephoto lenses tend to have a *shallower depth of field*. However, if no foreground subject is in your telephoto lens landscape photo, you probably don't have anything to worry about. Your iPhone will focus automatically on the distant horizon or other distant subject matter within your composition.

To focus your telephoto lens, or any of your iPhone lenses for that matter, all you need to do is what is often called the *long-press*. Follow along with this explanation even if you aren't near a landscape:

FIGURE 5-4:
The foreground
potted plant is
slightly out of
focus due to the
photographer not
manually
focusing the
iPhone's
telephoto lens.

REMEMBER

1. **Look at your composition and ask yourself whether any object within the scene requires manual focus.**

2. **Make note of the object or section of your composition that you want to force the camera to focus on, such as an object in the immediate foreground.**

3. **Press on that particular object or section and hold your finger for a few seconds.**

   When the little yellow square pops up underneath your finger, you've established focus.

Controlling focus and exposure with the AE/AF Lock

If a little yellow box that says AE/AF LOCK appears near the top of your photo, it means that the focus and exposure will remain constant, and the main focus point within your composition will be the area that you long-pressed with your finger.

TIP

Use the long-press AE/AF Lock technique for your landscape photos that include flowers or other objects in the immediate foreground. If those objects are important parts of the photo, focus on them, especially if you are using a telephoto lens for your landscape photo.

If your landscape photo is of distant mountains or other scenic shots that are far off, you don't need to worry about the long-press AE/AF lock technique. Simply take the photo, and your iPhone will look after giving you the focus sharpness that you need for a successful landscape photo, regardless of what iPhone lens you chose to use.

Lighting Considerations

Have you ever heard of photographers boasting about the *magic hour*? Magic hour is a term used by photographers and artists to signify the two times of day when the light from the sky is softer than usual and often excellent for landscape photography.

TIP

The reason that there are two magic hours is because we have both a sunrise and a sunset. When the light is low in the sky and also when it is below the horizon, the world takes on a peaceful, calm, and soft glow. It's magical!

Taking advantage of the magic hours

Before and after sunrise, you'll encounter the morning magic hour. Before and after sunset, you'll witness the beauty of the evening magic hour. But it gets even better! Did you know that the magic hour can be further divided into the greatest two colors in the world of photography?

REMEMBER

Magic hour is often subdivided into *golden hour* and *blue hour*. Blue hour, as illustrated in Figure 5-5, is approximately a half hour before sunrise and a half hour after sunset. Golden hour is roughly a half hour after sunrise and a half hour before sunset.

The world has a rich blueish glow before the sun rises, and as soon as the sun peaks over the distant horizon, as in Figure 5-6, the world becomes washed in the most wonderfully embracing warm, soft light.

Similarly, in the evening, we experience golden hour before sunset, and when the sun sets over the horizon the world reverts to the most electric and brilliant blue tone! It's a landscape photographer's dream.

There is only one small problem with both magic hour morning and evening time slots: They disappear too fast! If only we could extend the duration a bit more to have even longer landscape photo shoots. As you've probably guessed, making use of the two magic hours per day will dramatically increase your landscape photography prowess.

Magic hour is longer in duration the further away from the equator, going either northward or southward. In the Northern Hemisphere, the sun stays low to the horizon, giving soft magic hour light in late fall and early winter. For the Southern Hemisphere, magic hour is extended in duration around the months of June and July due to the sun staying low along the earth's horizon (from our perspective). Locations at or near the equator have a short magic hour due to the sun setting quickly, and pretty much straight from the sky directly down to the horizon.

The golden portion of magic hour is largely created by sunlight reflecting off of atmospheric particles, such as dust, smoke, and pollution. The more of these particles during golden hour, the warmer the sky will appear.

Here's a little landscape photography hint: If you live in North America, take a trip to Canada in the late autumn to early winter. Regardless of where you live in the world, by taking a trip farther North around the December solstice for those in the Northern Hemisphere, or farther South around the June solstice for those in the Southern Hemisphere, you'll encounter far more magic hour opportunities simply because the sun remains lower in the sky throughout the day. Lower sun in the sky throughout the day often equals soft and warm light, which is perfect for your iPhone landscape photography!

Timing magic hour

So, you are now a master at timing your next landscape photography adventure. All you need to do is set your alarm and get a good night's sleep. Arrive at your chosen location about an hour before sunrise, and you'll have set yourself up for photographic success.

Every iPhone has a built-in Weather app, and it conveniently tells you when the sun rises and sets for your home city or any world-wide destination that you add. Figure 5-7 shows the iOS Weather app, and how Sunrise is noted in your local time.

The iOS App Store has some excellent magic hour apps that were created for landscape photographers. Figure 5-8 show two examples derived from an iOS App Store search for the terms *magic hour.*

Try the following apps that are either free to download with optional in-app purchases or with an upfront fee:

>> Magic Hour, by elfinda apps

>> Alpenglow: Golden Hour Times, by Andrew Yates

>> Helios –Magic Hour Calculator, by Matic Conradi

FIGURE 5-7:
Check out your
iPhone's Weather
app for sunrise
times.

FIGURE 5-8:
Many iOS apps
help you time
magic hour for
your location.

Gear Considerations

Professional landscape photographers very rarely take photos without a tripod, as much of their work is done in the low-light hours of early morning or dusk. In addition, they prefer to work with certain lenses over others. This section helps you with both accessory gear and lens choices.

Steadying your iPhone camera with a tripod

The iPhone is remarkably adept at creating a sharp photo without a tripod. However, if you have access to a tripod, why not make the most out of those amazingly small yet sharp iPhone lenses?

Smartphone holders are usually plastic devices that clamp to your iPhone and screws onto your tripod's head plate. You can purchase these holders at pretty much any camera store and anywhere online. Search or ask for a "smartphone holder for a tripod." The online photographic company Neewer makes great quality tabletop tripods and mobile device clamps, as do the namebrand tripod companies, such as Manfrotto and Slik.

Most mobile photographers make use of two styles of stabilization depending on how much weight they can carry on their photo shoot. A lightweight option is a tabletop tripod with a mobile device clamp. As you can see on the left side of Figure 5-9, this option is not the best for landscape photographers as the small tripod requires a fairly flat, raised stable platform.

The option on the right of Figure 5-9 is much better for iPhone landscape photographers as it makes use of a normal sized tripod. As a landscape photographer, you'll have many more composition options if you use a larger tripod with the mobile device clamp attached to your tripod's head plate.

One of the biggest complaints that photographers have when talking about tripods is the inconvenience of carrying one around and also the extra weight when walking toward their scenic lookout. You can ease your burden if this sounds like you! Make sure that you choose a lightweight full-size tripod (either expensive carbon fiber or cheap plastic) and also keep your tripod in the trunk of your car.

Plastic tripods can get weighted down with your camera bag or anything else that has some weight if you're concerned about tripod stability. As for convenience, by keeping your tripod in your car, you'll be more inclined to use it when you drive by the next breathtaking landscape scene!

The best time to make use of a tripod is when the light is low, such as early morning and evening.

FIGURE 5-9:
Two different
tripod setups
often used by
mobile
photographers.

Choosing which lens to use (for multilens iPhones)

If you have a multilens iPhone, you may be wondering what the best lens for landscape photography is. With the advent of the triple-lens iPhone 11 Pro, iPhone photographers now have what is called an *ultra wide* lens. The ultra wide view is a favorite of landscape photographers as it packs the most amount of landscape scene into a single picture. Think of the blades of grass directly in front of your lens, PLUS the distant mountain range miles in the background. The ultra wide lens will be able to fit it all in.

If you have an earlier model iPhone you're not left out! The normal wide-angle view on any iPhone model is still fantastic for landscape photography.

REMEMBER

Regardless of what lenses you have on your iPhone, the bottom line is this: Practice choosing the widest angle that your particular iPhone model allows for. Landscape scenes practically beg for wide angle lenses! And when you print out your landscape for framing on the wall, you'll be happy you chose to go wide.

The ultra wide lenses on the iPhone 11 series, and most likely future iPhone models, have a look similar to the photo shown in Figure 5-10.

The photo shown in Figure 5-11 represents the iPhone's standard wide angle lens, which in various iterations has been with every iPhone since the original iPhone camera.

FIGURE 5-10:
The ultra wide
lens view,
included with all
11 series iPhone
models.

FIGURE 5-11:
The wide lens
view, included
with all iPhone
models.

The Figure 5-12 landscape photo is an example of what the telephoto lens view looks like. The telephoto lens visually pulls in distant objects to make them appear larger in the frame.

FIGURE 5-12:
The telephoto lens view makes distant landscape objects appear larger in your camera frame.

REMEMBER While there is never anything wrong with using a telephoto lens for landscape photography, keep in mind that most landscape photos tend to look better with a wider view rather than a telephoto view. Therefore, you may be inclined to use your wide or ultra wide lenses for most of your landscapes.

Photography Tips for Your Next Outing

Landscape photography requires great light, a stable iPhone, and also a composition that shows off the scene the best way possible. The word *composition* describes how photographers and painters present their chosen scene within the boundaries of their camera frame or painter's canvas. This section introduces and explains how the Rule of Thirds can help you compose your landscapes like a pro.

Applying the Rule of Thirds for better compositions

For better landscape compositions, you can add grid lines to your screen. Grid lines are like a tic-tac-toe grid overlaid on your camera screen so thatyou can create both straight photos and also follow the Rule of Thirds. If you haven't heard of the Rule of Thirds, then this section will almost guarantee that you'll come home with stunning landscape photographs. To activate your camera's grid lines, refer to Chapter 3.

TIP

The classic Rule of Thirds landscape scene is the lower one-third of your composition being land. The middle one-third section is entirely water. And finally, the top one-third of the composition is, you guessed it, the sky! Figure 5-13 shows a simple yet effective division of thirds, which you can mimic with your own photos.

FIGURE 5-13: An example of a traditional Rule of Thirds composition including land, water, and sky segmented into horizontal thirds sections.

There you have it . . . the Rule of Thirds explained in a few paragraphs. But don't feel limited to just land, water, and sky. You can also do a one-third and two-third split like in Figure 5-14: Maybe the bottom one-third of your landscape is a lovely Japanese garden at dusk, and the top two-thirds of your photo is a dramatic cloud-filled night sky.

FIGURE 5-14:
An example of a "lower one-third, upper two-thirds" composition.

Or you could alter that Rule of Thirds composition! Think about the bottom two-thirds of your composition being the Japanese garden, and the top one-third of your composition is the blue sky, similar to Figure 5-15.

You can mix and match the Rule of Thirds in a few different ways depending on your scene. And if you don't know what to do, why not take as many Rule of Thirds combinations as you can? Who knows, maybe they will all turn out to be frame-worthy gems.

When you hold your iPhone in the horizontal position (which is common for landscapes), Figure 5-16 is an example of what an iPhone 11 series screen should look like. Note that the grid lines in this sample screenshot are accentuated for illustrative purposes only. Your grid lines will look a bit thinner.

Using the Self Timer option for shake-free photos

One more simple step, and you'll be good to go. Your iPhone has what is called a *self-timer,* which allows you to press the shutter button, then let go of your iPhone, and then three or ten seconds later the iPhone will automatically take your photo. This delay is perfect for landscape photography, as it keeps your photo from being shaky due to you touching your iPhone while pressing the shutter button.

FIGURE 5-15:
An example of a "lower two-thirds, upper one-third" composition.

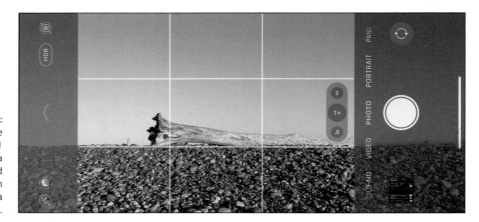

FIGURE 5-16:
The appearance of an iPhone 11 series camera screen with grid lines when composing a landscape photo.

When you're photographing with a tripod, use the self-timer and set it to three seconds. Because you're not physically touching the iPhone as the picture is being taken, your photo should be good and sharp.

REMEMBER

To start the self-timer for X series iPhones and earlier, simply tap on the little stopwatch icon located on the left of your screen. If you're holding your iPhone vertically, the icon is located at the top of your screen. For 11 series iPhones tap the top-middle arrow icon to reveal the camera's extra features, and then choose the stopwatch-looking self-timer icon.

Chapter **6**

Shooting Sports Photography

I f you have zero interest in sports, please don't finish this book without reading this chapter. Even though the theme is sports photography, I include a wealth of information that actually spans almost all photography genres!

When most people hear the term sports photography, they automatically discount themselves because they don't have the large and expensive pro photo gear that they see at stadium events or rink-side at high-level hockey games. Don't be dismayed! This chapter is for you, and it's written for what most people want to capture: their granddaughter at the high school basketball finals, their teenager trying out for the cycling team, or their best friend proudly finishing his first half marathon.

So, think of this chapter as a way to record life's wonderful friends and family memories that just happen to be sports related! These tips and techniques can help you build up a wealth of great photos that will serve as precious memories and also be of a high enough quality for publishing or printing.

Camera Considerations

When you think of sports photography, one of the first considerations that come to mind is the complexity of photographing a fast-moving person. Whether your subject is racing a bike, within a race car, or shooting hoops, *getting the shot* can certainly be challenging at times.

TIP

Because of that challenge, it's best to set your camera up for BURST MODE, which allows you to capture many photos in rapid succession, one after the other. With so many photos to choose from when reviewing the burst series, you can simply choose the best image out of all the options.

Take a look at Figure 6-1, which includes a soon-to-be-taken volleyball photo using an iPhone 11. Instead of just taking one image, the photographer put his thumb on the circular shutter release button and then slid his thumb downward to initiate the Burst mode photo capture. If he was taking a vertical photo, then it would be a slide to the left.

FIGURE 6-1:
Tap and then slide the shutter button down for Burst mode photo capture.

In Figure 6-2, you can see that the photographer took seven photos and then stopped the burst photo capture by removing his thumb from the shutter release button.

FIGURE 6-2:
Let go of the circular shutter button when you feel you've take enough Burst mode photos.

If you're using an iPhone that is an earlier model than the 11 series, you have it easy. Simply press and hold your shutter release button for as long as you like. The longer you hold the button, the more photos you will be taking of your sports scene. While you're taking the burst photo, you will see a little numerical counter ascending with the number of photos that you're capturing in real-time.

When you're ready to select the best image from the many photos within the burst, go to your iPhone's Photos app. After flipping through each image in the burst, you can choose to keep just one photo or as many photos as you like. For details on how to choose the best photo from a burst series, refer to Chapter 2.

REMEMBER

Gear Considerations

Pro sports photographers arguably use the largest and most expensive camera gear within the world of professional photography. That level of gear is necessary for their end-needs, which is high resolution, tack-sharp magazine and billboard quality photos. To capture amateur sports or just a backyard hockey game with your neighborhood friends, your iPhone will be up to the task.

The following sections cover optional gear choices that may help you in your sports photography adventures. Keep in mind, however, that none of these items are mandatory. You can capture great sports photos with just your iPhone!

TIP

A tough iPhone protective case

Sports gear goes through a lot of abuse because of radical temperature shifts and also the risk of dropping gear due to fast action. Shown in Figure 6-3, an iPhone case may keep your iPhone safe from that poorly aimed slapshot.

An iPhone screen protector

If your iPhone case doesn't come with its own clear plastic screen protector, take your iPhone to your local electronics store and ask for a durable stick-on screen protector. The screen protector will keep your iPhone's glass safe in case you drop it on a hard surface.

A monopod for steadier sports photos

A *monopod* is like a tripod but with just one leg instead of three. Sports photographers keep the monopod industry going! Whereas tripods are bulky and not convenient for sports photographers, monopods allow for a small footprint and will provide much more stability than hand-holding your iPhone.

A foldable camping seat

If you can get off the bleachers and closer to the action, try to capture your photo from a low position. This position will allow you to relax by sitting down, but more importantly make the athletes appear much grander and more powerful.

Battery packs or battery cases

If your sport is in the winter, bring along a battery pack. Cold weather can deplete your iPhone's battery much quicker than warmer temperatures.

Apple makes its own battery pack cases for most of its current iPhone lineup, such as in Figure 6-4. You'll notice the slight bump in the case, which holds the extra battery.

You can also just bring along a USB battery pack that is available at almost all camera and electronics stores. These packs can fit in your pocket and will give you a few more hours of cold weather usage when plugged into your iPhone.

FIGURE 6-4:
Extend your iPhone's battery life in the cold with a battery pack or battery pack case.

Touch-sensitive gloves in cold weather

Most clothing stores that sell winter clothes include gloves where the thumb, fore, and middle finders are touch sensitive. Touch sensitive means that you can freely use your phone while wearing gloves during cold days.

A telephoto lens attachment for distant athletes

Your iPhone may have a 2x telephoto lens, but if not, the photo accessory company olloclip is a world leader in creating attachment lenses for iPhones. Shown in Figure 6-5, a telephoto attachment lens will allow you to visually get closer to the athletes if they're far away from your camera, such as when you're in a stadium and your child is far off on the soccer field.

The more telephoto options you have (optical zoom + clip on telephoto + digital zoom), the easier it will be to capture a close-up of your favorite athlete.

FIGURE 6-5:
An *olloclip* telephoto lens attachment is useful for sports photography.

Lighting Considerations

You can do sports photography in the most diverse lighting situations. You may be photographing with mercury-vapor lights in a hockey arena in the morning and then stunningly beautiful evening light on the last ski run down the slopes. The following sections offer a few tips to help you maximize your lighting artistic and technical skills.

Photographing into the setting sun

Photographing into the sunset adds a sense of artistry to sports photography.

Keep in mind that it really only works well when the sun is just above the horizon, such as in Figure 6-6.

Photograph athletes into the sun only when the sun is very low to the horizon.

Using your Portrait mode

Sports photography almost always contains at least one portrait of the athletes or participants. So why not make them look their very best by using the Portrait mode? As in Figure 6-7, you will have a soft, pleasing blur behind your athletes.

For details on the Portrait mode and how to access it, check out Chapter 2. The process is the same, except that you're not using your selfie camera, but rather your back-facing camera.

FIGURE 6-7:
A normal photo
on the left, and a
portrait photo
with background
blur on the right.

Using shadows for a fine art sports photography look

There is no reason why sports photography can't cross over to the world of fine art once in a while. To easily do this, simply look for opportunities to capture athletes' shadows as they zoom past you.

This technique works best with direct sun rather than on overcast days. When the light is low to the horizon, be on the lookout for walls that cast the shadow similar to Figure 6-8. When the light is high in the sky, photograph the athletes' shadows being cast on the ground.

TIP

Creating silhouette sports photos

There is a huge demand for artistic sports photography for magazine cover shots. Take a look at Figure 6-9, which shows the black-and-white silhouette of a sports fishing participant. While this type of image may not work in the main article pages, silhouettes are visually powerful and are often used for promotional print or web design.

To create this type of photo, make sure that the sun is behind the athlete and then use one of the high contrast filters (see Chapter 2). Feel free to choose either color or black and white based on the intended usage of the photo.

TIP

FIGURE 6-8:
Infuse a sense
of fine art
photography into
your sports
images by
capturing an
athlete's shadow.

FIGURE 6-9:
Silhouette photos
are very
eye-catching and
great for sports
promotional
material.

Photographing during golden hour

Golden hour photography is not just for landscape photos! While it's not always possible due to scheduling, try your best to plan your outdoor sports photography when the light is low to the horizon. This low light will give your sports photos a stunningly warm and appealing look similar to the runners in Figure 6-10.

TIP

Go to Chapter 5 to find out more about the best times of the day to create images during golden hour. In a nutshell, about a half hour after sunrise and approximately a half hour before sunset make for the warmest looking photographs.

FIGURE 6-10:
When possible, photograph outdoor sports during golden hour.

Trusting your iPhone to produce accurate colors

If you ever hear photographers insist that you need to know the Kelvin scale or you need to understand every white balance setting before photographing indoor arenas and gymnasiums, don't listen to them. While it's true that professional photographers will often fine-tune their DSLR or mirrorless cameras to the exact technical color temperature of the overhead lights, you can rest assured that your iPhone has you covered.

In Figure 6-11, the iPhone had a pretty good idea of what type of artificial light was illuminating the gymnasium, and it adjusted the color of the photo accordingly. The term *white balance* refers to how your iPhone shows color along a blue and yellow scale (sometimes called *color balance*). Your iPhone's camera is always interested in making people look good, so it will automatically alter the color of a photo to best match human skin tone or interior and exterior spaces.

FIGURE 6-11:
Your iPhone will
automatically
choose the best
white balance to
give you accurate
colors.

Photography Tips for Dynamic Sports Photos

As with all photographic genres, sports photography has its own set of best practices. I selected the tips and techniques in the following sections to specifically help you with creating better iPhone sports photos, and as quickly and easily as possible.

Using the Rule of Thirds

In Figures 6-12 and 6-13, you see that there are two acceptable ways to frame-up your photo or crop your photo afterward. The upper horizontal Rule of Thirds line can either lay over the horizon as in Figure 6-12, or it can be raised a bit to meet the right-vertical line to create an intersecting point on the athlete's head as in Figure 6-13. Both of these compositions are acceptable. Also, notice how the runner is running *into* the picture space? Try not to center the runner. Rather, have the athlete enter the composition for a better sense of visual flow.

Panning your camera to create motion blur

A *panning* type photo means that you physically move your camera from left to right, or right to left, to follow a fast-moving athlete. Depending on how bright it is outside, you can usually create some pretty cool sports photos that border on fine art or abstract photography.

Take a look at Figure 6-14. Can you see that everything has forward motion blur except a few of the Canadian maple leaf stickers and a part of the athlete? A successful panning photo is one that conveys a sense of speed. You want your viewers to feel that they are there, in person, experiencing the rush of forward motion.

As long as one section is sharp, all the rest can be blurry. If everything is blurry, just press Delete and try again. Follow the athlete with your camera, moving your arms at the same speed, and take the photo mid-pan. This technique should produce a blurred background with some parts of the athlete remaining sharp.

FIGURE 6-14:
A good panning shot shows a sense of motion, and has at least one section of the image sharp, with the rest blurred in a directional manner.

Choosing the best-looking stride

All good running photos require that the athlete shows a good *stride*, which means that they have good form, and their legs appear to be in a classic running position. A great example of stride is Figure 6-15 where the image on the left has an unattractive stride, and the photo on the right has a good looking, or *classic*, stride.

It's easy to capture the perfect stride for any of your running photos, whether they be for the next marathon or your child running in the backyard. Simply set your camera to Burst mode, as explained earlier in this chapter in the "Camera Considerations" section, and then pick the photo with the best-looking stride.

FIGURE 6-15:
Choose a burst
photo where the
runner has a
good-looking
stride like the
photo on the
right.

But that's not all! If you're photographing a track and field meet and are photo-graphing at a right angle to the athlete, choose a burst photo where the athlete appears to be suspended in mid-air. This is a classic sports photographer trick that shows a sense of speed, agility, and a winner's attitude.

REMEMBER

This technique usually only works when it's sunny out, as it's the shadow below the runner that shows that neither of her feet are touching the ground. Figure 6-16 gives you an example of how the shadow looks and how it provides a sense of lev-ity to the sports photo.

FIGURE 6-16:
On a sunny day,
you can choose a
burst photo
where the runner
isn't touching the
ground.

Photographing from a lower position

As with fashion photography, it's often better for you, as the photographer, to position yourself lower than the height of the athlete. If your mobility allows for it, kneel or crouch down to a lower position while photographing the athlete moving toward or past you. This lower position makes the athlete look more impressive, both physically and metaphorically.

Packing a small foldable camp seat can help you comfortably get low, so you can photograph from a low position without hurting your knees. The snowboarder in Figure 6-17 looks more impressive because the photographer was both down the slope a little, as well as photographing from a waist-height position.

FIGURE 6-17: Try to photograph athletes from a lower position, which makes them look more impressive.

Creating contrast between athlete and background

While not always realistic due to the fact that you can't control athletes, when possible, situate yourself so that the background visually favors the athlete's face and upper body area. Figure 6-18 shows a side-by-side example of this technique. Take a look at the photo on the left side of the Figure 6-18. The photographer chose to position himself so that the snowboarder's light skin tone would be contrasted against the dark background of the trees. On the right side of Figure 6-18, you can see that the snowboarder's face loses a bit of prominence due to the snow being a similar luminosity as her skin tone.

For darker skinned athletes, the reverse would apply. If possible, you may want to search out a position where you can photograph that particular athlete with more of a lighter toned background.

REMEMBER

Regardless of skin tone or color, what you as a sports iPhone photographer want to do is make your athlete look the very best possible. And one way to do that is to find a composition where your athlete's face doesn't get lost and muddled with the background. Think contrast!

Photographing athlete group photos

Have you ever been asked to photograph a large group of people with your iPhone? It's not easy! The following tips can help you create those sports memories that in the future will end up being a valued historic record of you and your athletic friends:

>> If it's sunny outside, position your group so that the sun illuminates their faces instead of their backs.

>> If it's cloudy or overcast, compose your group to include the surrounding track, rink, field, or court. The background will provide context for your viewer.

» If you have enough people to need two or three rows for the group picture, try to find a position where you as the photographer can be higher than the group, such as in Figure 6-19. This higher position allows for all faces to be included and also shows off the sports field or location that you're in.

» Use Burst mode to take four or five rapid photos. Burst mode allows you to choose the photo where everyone looks good. Inevitably, at least one person will be blinking in a large group photo.

FIGURE 6-19:
Try to photograph large groups from a higher position to include all faces.

Chapter **7**

Saving Memories through Family and Individual Portraiture

P hotographing your family members not only provides an immediate sense of joy, but it also serves as an important historical record for many future generations. Think of all the family portraits that we enjoy looking at from the late 1800s onward, contemplating how life must have been so different back then.

So, as a recorder of your family's history, think of yourself as having a moral duty to photograph your family for the sake of creating a visual historical record. Many future generations will appreciate and value your work. How's that for a responsibility? You will do a wonderful job capturing family memories, especially after going through this chapter.

In this chapter, you discover many individual tips and techniques to artistically and technically create group, individual, and portrait family photos.

Camera Considerations

Family photos, whether group, individual, or portrait style, are easy to create due to your iPhone's reliance on Artificial Intelligence (AI). A lot of hidden calculations go on in a split second within your iPhone's computer to help you get a shot that you can be proud of. Still, many aspects of family photos are certainly your own responsibility. In this section, you explore your camera and how to use it for better family images.

Portrait mode pros and cons

In Chapter 4, you discover how to activate Portrait mode and how it is really great for creating a pleasing background blur behind your subject's head.

Portrait mode is fantastic for family photography, but it does have its limitations. Take a look at the photo in Figure 7-1. Because the kids were moving around with so many quick movements, it was difficult for the iPhone to capture them within Portrait mode. Because they wouldn't stay still while playfully fighting for the tasty well-water, the normal Photo mode was the better choice.

FIGURE 7-1:
Action family photos require the normal Photo mode instead of Portrait mode.

The photo within Figure 7-2 is a different story . . . as the kids were sitting perfectly still on the window ledge, they were prime candidates for Portrait mode. The cropped-in view of Figure 7-3 shows the pleasing blur that the iPhone applied to the stone building behind the kids. This type of family photo, namely everyone being still, is perfect for Portrait mode's dreamy background blur.

FIGURE 7-2: Portrait mode is perfect for motionless family photos and portraits.

Burst mode

Kids usually have boundless energy, and most often that energy comes out just when you want a calm, relaxed family portrait! Well, you may do better letting them run around wildly to get their energy out, while at the same time capturing action family photo memories. All you need to do is treat them like a sports team (see Chapter 6).

TIP

Your iPhone's Burst mode is the best bet for capturing kids running around, as you'll be able to choose the best photo out of a series of many images. Chapter 6, which is all about Sports iPhone photography, explains in detail how to activate Burst mode.

Figure 7-4 shows an example of a Burst mode photo that included 15 consecutive photos back to back. Three out of those 15 photos were really good, and the rest were destined to the Trash bin.

FIGURE 7-3:
A cropped view of
the background
blur applied
behind the kids'
heads.

FIGURE 7-4:
Out of 15 Burst
photos, the
photographer
chose the three
best images.

You can select as many photos from your Burst series as you like or only your one favorite image. All you need to look out for is the way in which the kids look based on posture. Pick the image(s) where the kids appear active and engaged and trash the ones where their limbs are flailing and look awkward. Other than that, all other decision-making parameters are up to you. To find out how to activate Burst mode, refer to Chapter 6.

Self-timer

If the light is getting lower in the sky and you're using a tripod for a family portraiture session, why not maximize your sharpness by using your self-timer? An iPhone camera comes with a three- and ten-second countdown timer, which allows you to get into your own photo. But even if you aren't planning to be in the photograph, by using your three-second timer, you avoid touching the iPhone. With no touching during the photo-taking process, you have the potential for sharper images.

For more on self-timer setup, refer to Chapter 5. The less you touch your camera during the photo capture, the less chance of camera shake.

Follow these steps for an iPhone 11 series model, as shown in Figure 7-5:

1. **Tap the extra features arrow to display the timer icon.**

2. **Tap the timer icon and choose three seconds if you're the photographer.**

3. **Tap ten seconds if you're both the photographer and also need to run into the picture.**

   When you see a three- or ten- second timer icon appear on-screen, the photo is ready to be taken.

4. **Tap the white circular shutter release icon to take the photo.**

FIGURE 7-5:
Use the three-second timer when you're the photographer and the ten-second timer when you plan to be a part of the photo.

TIP

Professional portrait and wedding photographers often make use of candid photos to add a sense of warmth and fun to a photo shoot. Always capture candid photos of the portrait setup, prior to the formally composed family composition. Figure 7-5 shows a family preparing to get organized for a properly composed family iPhone photo, but the wacky positions they were in while getting ready actually became a family favorite! Don't ever be limited to the formal pose. Capture as many candid shots as possible during all stages of a family portrait session.

Gear Considerations

When tripods are mentioned, there's often a common and understandable reaction that goes something like this: "I know I should use a tripod for family photos, but they are such a hassle!!!"

Yes, it's true that carrying around a full-size tripod everywhere you go would be out of the question. However, a portable tabletop tripod would fit in any purse or even a large pocket. In Figure 7-6, I used a small tabletop tripod to photograph my family on the sandy beach below the rocks. Because the sun had already set, the use of a tripod similar to one in Figure 7-7 resting on a solid rock made for a sharp photograph.

FIGURE 7-6: Tabletop tripods work great when placed on stable surfaces, such as large rocks.

FIGURE 7-7:
Tabletop tripods
are convenient,
portable, and, as
long as there is a
stable surface like
a boulder, very
effective for
stable low-light
photography.

The type of tabletop tripod is really not that important. The ball-head is, however, quite important. From the left to right in Figure 7-7, you will see that only the middle tripod has an adjustable ball-head. The tripod on the left has limited flexibility due to spreading the tripod legs at various degrees, but it doesn't have a ball-head to allow for precise camera angles. Fortunately, the tripod on the left can easily be fitted with a ball-head, which can be sold separately.

The *puck* on the right is a mobile device holder that is meant for rotational videos and panoramic photographs. This type of holder is ideal for such niche uses, but not good enough for on-site family portraits.

What you're looking for in a tabletop tripod is three elements:

>> The legs

>> A ball-head that attaches to the legs

>> A mobile device holder or clamp that fits your iPhone to the ball-head

Sometimes all three of these elements are purchasable in one unit, and other times you may want to buy all three separately and assemble them together yourself.

TIP

Taller tripod legs may be a bit more useful when photographing from uneven surfaces, such as the large rock in Figure 7-6.

REMEMBER

Using a tripod for any photos that are in motion is a recipe for frustration! If your family members are moving around or you have antsy kids, just go hand-held and take as many photos as possible. At least one of them will probably work out just fine. But trying to follow them around while your iPhone is attached to a tripod will be more hassle than it's worth.

Lighting Considerations

If you've ever heard the maxim "Photography is all about light," you may be wondering about all the other aspects of photography that are not light related. What about gear? What about a good-looking subject? What about technical skill? Yes, all of those are pieces to the puzzle, but photography in its fundamental form is a game of manipulating light to create a desired photographic result.

To that end, this section is chock-full of lighting tips to help you present your family members in the best possible manner. Everyone wants to look good in family photographs, and you can be that rare shining light that presents your family in a way that they can be proud of.

Underexposing your portraits for extra drama

If the sun is soft and low, your family member portrait session can be really successful simply by asking him or her to look into the light. One fantastic way to add drama to your portraiture is to underexpose your photo just before you take the picture. *Underexpose* means that you make the overall photo a bit darker. The combination of your model looking into the light plus underexposure creates a really dramatic end result.

WARNING

Looking into the sun, even for a second or two, is dangerous. You can get the same results by asking your model to look in the general direction of the setting or rising sun, but obviously not directly into it. Also, feel free to tell them to keep their eyes closed until you count down from 3 to 1. Then when they briefly open their eyes and smile, you can take the photo before it gets too uncomfortable for them.

Figure 7-8 shows a family member portrait session in front of a dark European doorway. This type of lighting creates an artistic portrait, and you can easily re-create it! If you can plan a similar looking portrait session, and you choose an artistic looking dark background, follow these simple steps to underexpose your portrait:

FIGURE 7-8:
Steps to
underexpose
a portrait for
added drama.

1. **Choose a dark background such as a wall or doorway.**

2. **Ask your model to look in the direction of the setting or rising sun so that their face is illuminated.**

3. **To make your photo artistically darker, tap and hold your finger on your subject's head until you see a yellow square appear and a yellow AE/AF LOCK icon appears at the top of your screen.**

4. **Remove your figure from the yellow square only briefly and then swipe your finger on-screen in a downward motion.**

    This step causes your photo to become darker, signified by a little yellow sun icon moving downward along a yellow slider graphic.

5. **When you've reduced the exposure of the photo to the extent that you like, remove your finger from the downward swiping motion.**

    Your photo will retain its new darker appearance.

TIP

This underexposure process also works in reverse! To make photos brighter, simply do the opposite. You will swipe upward instead of downward, which again will be signified by the little yellow sun icon moving up the yellow slider icon.

Looking out the window

Window light is truly amazing. In fact, the history of portrait and family photography is almost entirely based on north-facing window light. Before studio lighting was invented, photographers would choose photo studio locations based on large windows that faced north so that their window illumination would be soft and even.

Follow these simple steps to create your own window light portrait similar to Figure 7-9:

1. **Choose a window that doesn't have direct rays of sun shining in.**

2. **Have your model look out the window.**

3. **Choose either Portrait mode if you want background blur or normal Photo mode if you don't need background blur.**

4. **Take the photo when the window side of your model's face is illuminated and the nonwindow side of their face is a bit darker, which creates portrait drama.**

Photographing travel photos during blue hour

Travel family photos may seem a bit trivial during the actual trip, but keep in mind that decades later, those photos increase in sentimental value. Future generations will thank you for taking those trip photos!

To show off your vacation surroundings in the best possible light, choose to photograph your family members just after sunset. The sky will get bluer and bluer, and the city's electric lights will be the same luminosity (brightness) as the sky. This even illumination of both the sky and the artificial lights creates a soft and lovely looking background to use as a travel portrait location.

Figure 7-10 shows a family photo where the girls are illuminated by both the remaining skylight and the artificial streetlights. This combination of light is usually pleasing for portraits as it shows off the city streets really well and also doesn't produce many shadows on the faces of your family members.

REMEMBER

Blue hour photography, which I discuss in greater detail in Chapter 5, is usually a short window of time that starts just after sunset and lasts for about a half hour. So be ready, as the light will change quickly. Of course, you can also plan for morning blue hour, which is about a half hour prior to sunrise.

FIGURE 7-10:
Blue hour family
portraits show off
your family
members and the
city with a soft
and pleasing
appearance.

Using shadows to create pictograms

If you have a sunny day with harsh, direct sunlight, why not practice creating pictograms? A loose definition for a *pictogram* in the world of people photography is the expression of an idea created by simple compositions. These compositions are often abstract in nature and usually don't show the people creating the pictographic image.

Figure 7-11 shows two sisters creating a heart shape based on their arm placements. While it's true that you can't tell who is in the photo, the goal is simply to promote an idea. In this case, the idea is the bond that these two sisters share. The different types of pictograms you can create are limited only to your imagination and the type of lighting that you have to work with.

Making use of silhouettes for dramatic portraits

WARNING

One really big mistake that a lot of iPhone photographers make is feeling that every family photo needs to see the details of each person clearly. This is not always needed! Often, you can create extra drama when you can see only the silhouette of your loved ones.

Figure 7-12 is a good example of two sisters and their friends having fun at a water park. If the photographer walked to the other side of the park, the sun would have illuminated the girls perfectly. However, the photographer chose *backlighting,* which is a type of light where only the backs of the kids are illuminated. *Backlighting* means, of course, that you won't see much or any detail, but you don't need to. Silhouette-style backlighting adds an artistic element to your family photos that are almost always attractive.

TIP

This effect is best accomplished when you include the rising or setting sun within your composition.

Placing family members in the shade for even light

Harsh, direct sunlight portraiture usually only works out well for supermodels and young people who have really great complexions. For the rest of us, portraiture is best done in the shade, on overcast or cloudy days, or a mix of both.

Figure 7-13 shows a Portrait mode photo that is both under the shade of a tree and also with the soft light of an overcast sky. Both of these elements come together to create soft and pleasing family portraits.

FIGURE 7-12:
To create silhouette family photos, let your models be between the rising or setting sun and your iPhone. The effect is increased if the sun appears within your composition.

FIGURE 7-13:
Choose overcast days and/or shady areas for family portraits.

Did you notice that even though the man in the photo in Figure 7-13 was wearing a ball cap, no deep shadow appears under the hat? On sunny days, a ball cap would cast an unappealing dark shadow across the face, which rarely works well for portraits.

Photographing from behind with low sunlight

Seeing only the backs of people is not usually the best way to create family photos. There is, however, an exception. Ask your family members to walk away from you in the direction of the rising or setting sun. What you will usually get is a pleasing golden rim of light that traces around them, similar to Figure 7-14.

FIGURE 7-14: Photograph people as they walk away from you using low sunlight.

You may be wondering how this technique is different than in Figure 7-12. The placement of the family members is very similar, but the big difference is that in Figure 7-12 the setting sun is included in the photo, which allows for a silhouette, but in Figure 7-14 the sun is not directly included in the composition.

TIP

When the sun isn't included, you will usually be able to see detail on your models. When the sun is included, your models will usually be shown as a silhouette.

Photography Tips for Your Next Portrait Session

Portraiture is one of the trickiest genres of iPhone photography because you're dealing with people who naturally want (and sometimes demand) that you make them look amazing. This desire, of course, is understandable. The following sections explain tools at your disposal to present your family members in the best light possible!

Photographing from a lower position

When you look through any fashion magazine, you can be assured that the photographer has taken the photo of the model from a lower perspective. Fashion photographers are almost always photographing from their knees or in a crouched position, as this lower angle portrays the models in an empowered, authoritative manner.

You can make use of the fashion photography low-angle portrait technique, too! Simply photograph them whereby your iPhone camera lens is aimed at their midsection. This technique make them appear taller and more empowered, as in this Figure 7-15 family portrait taken in the famous bamboo groves of Kyoto, Japan.

FIGURE 7-15: Photograph your younger family members from a lower position to create a more empowered look.

Choosing black and white
for fine art portraits

In Chapter 2, you discover a quick and easy way to take your photo in black and white. When you capture that perfect photo that you know will be a family favorite that lasts through the generations, why not take a second photo using one of the black-and-white filters? Of course, you can always create black-and-white conversions during the photo-editing process, but if your family members are staying still or sleeping as in Figure 7-16, you will have plenty of time to snap a second photo using an artistic black-and-white option.

FIGURE 7-16: If you have time, take a second family portrait in black and white to add an artistic touch to your image.

Trying forced perspective techniques
for fun family pics

Forced perspective photos are images where it looks like a person is as large as a huge building, such as the church in Figure 7-17. Creating them is easy:

1. **Find a large and iconic building, such as a church or, if in Italy, the Instagram-favorite Leaning Tower of Pisa!**

2. **Find a location where the distant background building has the same light as the light that is illuminating your model.**

    This step is important. If the person is in shadow and the building in direct sunlight (or vice versa), this technique won't work.

FIGURE 7-17:
Forced
perspective
photos make
people appear to
be as large as tall
buildings.

3. **Crouch down in a low position.**

4. **Ask your family member to place their hand so that it appears that they're holding the top of the distant large building.**

TIP

For a fun sampling of forced perspective photos, do an Instagram search for Leaning Tower of Pisa. Visitors have produced these illusions in some really creative ways! You can do the same using locations much closer to home.

WARNING

Don't use Portrait mode for forced perspective portraits. Only use the normal Photo mode, as you want to avoid any background blur.

Using the Thirds grid for environmental portraits

All iPhones come with an option to overlay a Rule of Thirds grid onto your camera's screen. This grid helps you compose photos with greater accuracy and straightness. (To find out how to make the grid visible, go to Chapter 5.)

The term *Environmental Portraiture* can be loosely described as photographing people or pets within either their living environment or their favorite places. Take Figure 7-18, for example. This East Coast of Canada location is a favorite for this family member, so when visiting, it's important to include a lot of that environment within the composition.

FIGURE 7-18:
The Rule of Thirds
grid helps you
compose
environmental
portraits.

The grid allows you to compose your image in such a way that looks balanced. In Figure 7-18, you can see that the sand occupies the lower horizontal third, and the upper horizontal two-thirds is occupied by the attractive rocks.

REMEMBER

Keep in mind that the Rule of Thirds doesn't need to be slavishly followed . . . it's simply a guide that traditionally looks good. But as you are the artist, feel free to compose as you like.

Creating humorous photos to keep the mood light

Have you ever woken up and felt that everything is wrong with the world? If so, you're not alone. However, a wonderful antidote to that emotion is the world of silly photos! Create and view as many funny photos as possible, as these gems always lighten the mood.

You can plan funny family photos, such as the chip bag on the right of Figure 7-19, or they can be completely spontaneous, such as a fun lunch at the ski lodge in Figure 7-20.

In a sense, you have a moral obligation to keep the word smiling. So get out there and create as many silly family photos as possible!

FIGURE 7-19:
Always be on
the lookout for
funny photo
opportunities.

FIGURE 7-20:
When kids are
spontaneously
acting silly, get
photographing!

Avoiding objects sticking out of people's heads

This is a common complaint: "Hey, I have a telephone pole coming out of my head!"

Well, to avoid the telephone pole coming out of your family member's head, or as in Figure 7-21 the vase of flowers, always double-check to make sure that everyone's head has a clean background.

TIP

Interestingly, by using Portrait mode for your family photos you can minimize this problem, as the background automatically becomes blurry.

Choosing to include mirrors in your compositions

Don't let a single moment pass you by! Always look for photo opportunities within every location that you are in and especially make use of elevator mirrors. You can create some unique photos within those multimirrored tiny spaces.

Elevator mirrors allow for a sense of abstract portraiture, especially when you compose in such a way that a person appears twice in the same photo as in Figure 7-22. You can either include yourself in them or simply move around a bit so that you're not included in any mirror reflection.

FIGURE 7-22: Mirrored elevators are great locations for unique family photos.

Including family member's interests

This family photography tip may seem overly simplistic and obvious, but it's amazing how many people neglect documenting their family involved in their hobbies and other interests. Sports usually gets a lot of screen time, but quieter endeavors are often neglected.

Each year as children or grandchildren grow up, try to get at least one photo of them doing or being involved in their favorite hobby, such as the young sketch artist shown in Figure 7-23. Their hobbies will most likely change over the years, and your visual record of them will be a highly cherished memory decades to come.

Avoiding overcast skies

Overcast skies are fantastic for portraiture, as the soft light produced by the cloud cover creates flattering portrait lighting. However, if you have the ability to compose your photo so that the overcast sky is not included in your family picture, you may end up with a more visually powerful final image.

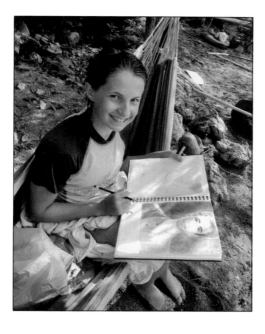

FIGURE 7-23: A simple example of showcasing and documenting a family member's drawing talent.

Take a look at Figure 7-24, which shows an overcast sky that doesn't really add any value to the photo. The image shown in Figure 7-25 allows the viewer to appreciate the people a bit more, as one less visual element in the image competes for your viewer's attention.

Think of it this way: A background should almost always support the subject. The subject matter in Figure 7-24 is the family, so they're the priority. If you reduce the amount of varied visual elements in the background, your viewer will probably linger on the people more instead of being distracted by non-essential visuals like an overcast sky.

REMEMBER

In saying that, however, keep in mind that wonderful blue skies, dramatic storm clouds, or sunsets are completely different. Dramatic skies often add to the family portrait, not take away from it. It's the definition-less and blah-looking overcast sky that is often best removed, as it really doesn't add visual value to the family being photographed.

TIP

You can avoid a distracting sky by zooming in or by cropping your photo afterward.

FIGURE 7-25:
If a sky doesn't
have any visual
value, either don't
include it or crop
it out later.

Combining family photos using the Layout app

A social media favorite that you may have seen on your Facebook feed is a grouping of multiple photos into one single image. If you'd like to share just one photo that includes four different scenes rather than share four separate photos, download the app called Layout from Instagram, which produces combined photos similar to Figure 7-26.

FIGURE 7-26: A typical four-photo layout that is saved as a single image file, suitable for social media uploading.

When opened, the app asks you to select your favorite multiple photos from your Photos collection, and the app takes care of assembling the photos with your input. When done creating your layout, you can save the newly created image to your Photos app camera roll and proceed to upload to your favorite social media platform.

Photographing from an aerial perspective

While there's value in photographing people from a lower perspective, which gives them a fashion-model type of appearance, this tip is the opposite: It's also valuable to photograph a family member from a higher angle, often called an *aerial perspective*. This situation is certainly the case when photographing newborns or small children, as in Figure 7-27.

Most likely, 90 percent of all photography in the world is taken at eye-level, which is probably about 5.5 feet or so off the ground. So why not buck the trend and take photos that are unique? Avoid the eye-level photos and use creative compositional angles, such as aerials, to create your family masterpieces.

Screenshot photos for family who are away

On a business trip and you miss your family? You can easily create your own family photos by using your iPhone's Facetime app! You'll end up with a screenshot photo similar to Figure 7-28.

FIGURE 7-28:
Use Facetime
video calling and
screenshots to
save photo
memories when
you are away.

To create a photo from your iPhone's screen, follow along with these easy steps:

1. **Open your Facetime app.**

2. **Video-call your family member.**

3. **When you see them on the video call, ask them to smile.**

4. **Do a screenshot, which saves that lovely smile to your Photos app.**

   A screenshot can be done very easily. For an iPhone X series model or later, press the volume up button on the left (when holding vertically) and the side button on the right at the exact same time. This will save your screen to your Photos app.

   On an iPhone 8, 7, or 6 series model, press the side button on the right and the Home button at the same time.

   On an iPhone SE, 5, or earlier model, press the top button and the circular home button at the same time.

IN THIS CHAPTER

» Using Portrait mode for nonhuman
  subjects

» Photographing travel cityscapes
  through hotel windows

» Minimizing clutter in your travel
  photos

» Choosing S-curve compositions when
  traveling

» Composing for equidistance

» Placing people with more space in
  front of them

Chapter **8**

Documenting Your Travel and Vacation in Pictures

Whether your travel or vacation adventure is across the world or to the next state, documenting your experiences will act as a highly valued time-capsule for future generations.

Do you value those old photo albums from generations past? They give us a glimpse into our family history, especially the fun photos taken by past family members when travelling or on vacation. So, do the same courtesy to our future generations and give them the opportunity for a sense of nostalgia many decades from now.

In this chapter, you discover pro tips for capturing the best of your travel and vacation photos. Never again will you bore your friends and family members back home with hundreds of soul-less snapshot photos of historic European buildings. You and your family are the stars of this show, and this chapter leads you down the path of travel photography greatness.

Camera Considerations

Travel photography is technically not very different than other genres of photography. Certain travel photography techniques, however, are somewhat unique to the travel photography genre. This section showcases a few examples of how you can operate your camera to benefit your diverse travel photography experiences.

Using Burst mode for moving subjects

For non-Europeans, the image of the European cyclist or simply a lone bicycle is a cliché, but still a lovely photo indulgence. When you see that wonderful grandmother or gentleman ride toward you on a classic Italian bicycle, choose Burst mode to guarantee the shot. (See Chapter 5 for more on Burst mode.)

Figure 8-1 shows the best photo chosen from a burst of eight photos. The reason this one was the best was because the cyclist's position was perfectly under the classic European window. Also, choose either the best stride (for people walking or running), or if on a bicycle or motorcycle, the best location of the subject in relation to the background.

WARNING

Check with local laws regarding photographing people without permission. The general rule for locations without such laws is that you don't photograph people in embarrassing or compromising situations. Maintain respect for your chosen subject. Also, you can't sell your travel photos of people for commercial purposes without a model release. Commercial purposes refer to an image of people being used to sell a product or a service without them knowing. Always be respectful and show local residents in the best possible light. See Chapter 10 to get more insight on how to photograph strangers in a way that retains dignity.

Capturing portraits with both Portrait and Photo modes

Travel photography with family members inevitably includes backgrounds of famous landmarks or quaint historic back alleys. If possible, try to capture two versions of each portrait: one with Portrait mode on for background blur, and the other without Portrait mode, using the normal camera on Photo mode. The reason this is valuable is because some famous landmarks and locations still look fantastic even blurred, and the blur makes your family member look great.

FIGURE 8-1: Burst mode is often used for sports, but it's also useful for any fast-moving subjects.

A good example of this is in Figure 8-2, which shows the famous Rogue Alley in Saint John, New Brunswick, Canada. With Portrait mode on, the background is blurred but still as attractive and appealing as ever.

Figure 8-3 is in the same location outside of Rogue Coffee, but this time the photo has no background blur due to a normal portrait using Photo mode.

TIP

To save time when you are in a rush, you can let one photo do double-duty. Just take one travel portrait using Portrait mode, and the background blur of that one portrait can be adjusted for full blur, or a sharp, no-blur background (see Chapter 4 to find out how to activate Portrait mode and how to adjust the level of background blur). Even though Chapter 4 discusses selfie Portrait mode, the instructions are identical for normal back-facing camera photography of your family member.

FIGURE 8-2:
Create travel
portraits with
Portrait mode
for pleasing
background blur.

FIGURE 8-3:
Take the same
photo without
background blur
using the normal
Photo mode.

Photographing nonportraits
in Portrait mode

When travelling, you often encounter flowers or budding trees that are not native to your own country. If you come across a wonderfully colorful or intricately designed flower or blossom, try this trick to take your travel photos to the next level:

1. **Switch to Portrait mode.**

2. **Pretend that the flower or blossom is a human face.**

3. **Tap on the face of the flower until a square icon is visible.**

   Ignore any warning that says "Move Farther Away."

4. **When the flower is in focus and the background is blurry, take the photo.**

Figures 8-4 and 8-5 are good examples of how you can capture a full cherry blossom tree, such as this one in Japan, but also get a really great portrait of the blossom by switching to Portrait mode. Keep in mind that this Portrait mode camera hack works best with late model iPhones.

FIGURE 8-4:
You can use
Portrait mode for
flowering trees
such as cherry
blossoms.

FIGURE 8-5:
Get close to a
blossom or
flower and
activate Portrait
mode for
background blur.

Choosing black and white for iconic locations

Multigenerational portraits in the context of travel or vacation photography create highly cherished memories and when printed are especially fantastic as wall art. Figure 8-6 shows a father and son walking through a famous European archway. This color photo is okay, but it has a few distractions, such as the yellow shed and red box. To transform this family travel photo into frame-worthy wall art, take the photo in black and white using one of the black-and-white filters, or convert the photo to black and white later on, as in Figure 8-7.

REMEMBER

Don't worry about missing out on the color version years down the road. When you take an iPhone photo in black and white, you can always revert to color at any future date.

WARNING

Keep in mind that the ability to revert to color is only possible if your photo stays within your iPhone's Photos app. If you send your black-and-white iPhone-captured photo to a third-party app for extra editing and then bring that photo back into the iPhone Photos app, your ability to revert to the color version will be lost. That's why most third-party apps give you the option to either make a copy or overwrite your original photo. Always choose to make a copy, which will retain your original photo within your Photos app.

FIGURE 8-6:
Color travel
photos
sometimes have
distractions that
detract from the
look and feel of
the scene.

FIGURE 8-7:
Choose black
and white for
multigenerational
artistic travel
photos.

Your third-party app edited photo will come into Photos as a copy. This is a good thing, as you will then have both your original iPhone created photo that can be reverted to color at any time and also your extra-edited photo. You will see two versions of the same photo within your Photos app. If you don't plan to use any third-party apps for editing, you can ignore this.

To find out how to capture a photo using a black-and-white filter, see Chapter 2.

Photographing cityscapes through windows

When travelling to a major city, ask your hotel for a room on an upper floor. You can create dramatic photos, both with iPhone and DSLR cameras, simply by placing your lens directly on the windowpane. Here are the steps to create brilliant travel cityscape photos.

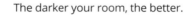

1. **Ideally choose a time before sunrise or after sunset to avoid windowpane reflections.**

2. **Turn off all lights in your hotel room.**

   The darker your room, the better.

3. **Dress with dark clothing to avoid reflections.**

4. **Orient your iPhone so that the lens end is closest to the glass.**

5. **If your scene allows for it, place your iPhone flush against the window.**

6. **With your lens touching or almost touching the glass window pane, take the photo.**

A lot of people who are into iPhone photography also have DSLR or mirrorless cameras, and the preceding steps are identical for larger cameras. Figure 8-8 shows a photographer with the tip of her lens actually touching the glass. The closer your lens is to the window pane, the less chance of reflections ruining your image.

Photographing travel scenes with the ultra wide lens

If you're the owner of an iPhone 11 Pro model, train yourself to choose the ultra wide-angle lens for travel street scenes. Most photographers assume that the ultra wide lens is primarily for landscape or architectural photography, but it's also a truly unique tool to present your travels in an unusual way.

FIGURE 8-8:
Get your lens as close to the glass as possible. Ideally, it should be physically touching the window pane.

Figure 8-9 shows a famous street in San Juan, Puerto Rico. Because it was photographed using the iPhone's ultra wide lens, the photo seems to feel stretched and unusual. That's because the ultra wide lens shows reality in a much different way than what the human eye sees. And because of this visual uniqueness, your photos will gain much more attention from viewers because of how novel your scene appears to be.

Getting detail in night scenes using Night mode

With the advent of the iPhone 11, Night mode allows you to extend your travel photography opportunities by helping you capture images at night. The nice thing about Night mode is that you don't need to do anything. Your iPhone will automatically switch to Night mode if it senses that the light is low enough to warrant the feature.

For those with iPhone 11 series models, test Night mode when the light gets lower in the sky or in your house. As in Figure 8-10, a yellow icon appears that displays how many seconds it will take for your iPhone to capture the night scene successfully.

FIGURE 8-9:
If you have an ultra wide-angle lens, use it for travel streetscapes for a very unique perspective.

FIGURE 8-10:
Night mode on iPhone 11 series models is indicated by a little yellow icon that comes on automatically.

Keep your iPhone as still as possible while the exposures are happening. A tripod is ideal, a stable platform is second best, and hand-held with your arms tucked into your rib cage should be fine if you have no other stability options.

If you don't see a yellow icon rather a white one without a time indicator, it means that your iPhone can get away without Night mode. You can force Night mode, however, simply by tapping on that white icon and manually choosing how many seconds you want Night mode to use for your image capture.

For new users of Night mode, don't worry about the white icon's manual options. Simply take your night photos allowing your iPhone to decide for you.

Choosing all three lenses for iconic scenes

The iPhone 11 Pro models have three lenses: the normal, wide, and ultra wide. If you own a Pro model, try to capture iconic scenes using all three lens choices. For example, if you're on a cruise and see a beautiful sunrise or sunset scene, find a location on the ship that allows you to capture the same scene with all three lens views.

Figure 8-11 is an example of a Caribbean sunrise of the exact same scene, but each photo turned out to be its own unique photograph. While you may not want to take three photos of every scene, at least the grand or iconic locations would be worthy of taking the time to capture with all three angles.

FIGURE 8-11: Use all three lenses for iconic scenes if you have an 11 Pro iPhone.

Gear Considerations

In our current digital age, we've been liberated from lack of knowledge (Google, Siri, Alexa), but enslaved to the need for a power socket! When you're travelling, a few extra gear items gain importance simply because you may be in unfamiliar environments that may or may not have power for your iPhone.

But power isn't the only thing to consider. In the following sections, you read about a few travel safety precautions, a tough yet good-looking iPhone travel bag, protecting your iPhone from water, and why selfie sticks are great for the lone traveler.

Extending your photography with battery packs

You can extend the battery life of your iPhone in two primary ways:

» Apple has its own protective Smart Battery Case that fits most iPhone models.

» Battery companies create power supplies that will charge your iPhone via a cable.

Either one of these options will probably be more than enough for most travelers, as modern iPhones usually last for at least a full day of average use. And then when you get back to your hotel at night, you can charge up for the next day.

Figure 8-12 is an example of my iPhone 11 Max Pro with the Apple Smart Battery Case and a supplementary battery pack for multiday camping adventures.

FIGURE 8-12:
The combination of an Apple Smart Battery Case and a battery pack will potentially extend your photography for multiple days without AC wall-socket power.

There are, however, power users who drain their iPhone batteries quickly due to intense RAW image processing and video usage. For them, an extra power supply is a wise choice, especially when far away from an urban environment with a lack of café power sockets.

If you plan on camping or going on a safari, you may actually want to double up on the extra power by choosing both the Smart Battery Case and a separate battery pack. This option would potentially keep you photographing for multiple days of average iPhone usage.

A rarely used but necessary third power option that backcountry adventurers keep in their backpacks is portable solar panels. This option may not be a practical, or even necessary, solution for most people, but for those who are travelling off-road for days on end, portable solar panels can be a lifesaver.

Packing a tabletop-sized tripod

A tripod isn't critical for travel photography, as most often you'll be with family and have enough baggage as it is. However, if you tend to pack light, any type of travel or tabletop tripod will do the trick.

Photographing or filming yourself with a selfie stick

If you don't want to pack a tripod on your next travel adventure, some selfie sticks actually come with three little legs that can fold out to act as a type of tripod. But the real value of selfie sticks for solo travelers is the ability to create selfie photos without having your arm extended within the picture.

Take a look at Figure 8-13. Normally when people take mobile device selfies, you can see that it's a selfie because of their extended arm in the picture, but in this example, it appears that the woman was posing for a normal photo taken by a friend. Consider a good quality selfie stick like the one in Figure 8-14 made by CliqueFie and sold by Apple within the Apple Store.

Purchasing the best protective case for your needs

Will your travel adventures include water? Even though late model iPhones have decent water resistance, it's best not to tempt fate. To that end, a waterproof case and floatable lanyard are indispensable.

FIGURE 8-13:
Solo travelers and
influencers can
create better
selfies using selfie
sticks, avoiding
their extended
arm in the
picture.

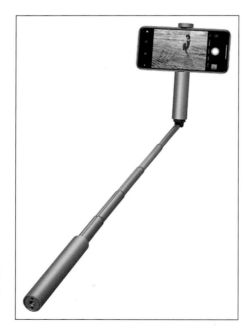

FIGURE 8-14:
A portable and
good quality
selfie stick made
by CliqueFie.

Figure 8-15 shows a scene where parents are most likely to lose their iPhones to the depths of the river or lake. The kids are having a blast, Dad looks over the boat to snap a photo, and the rogue wave makes him drop his iPhone and it's gone forever. Companies like Catalyst create both waterproof iPhone cases and floating lanyards, shown in Figure 8-16. This combo allows your iPhone to float safely until you can circle back to pick it out of the water.

FIGURE 8-15:
A common scenario: Leaning over the water to take a photo, potentially dropping your iPhone.

FIGURE 8-16:
A Catalyst brand floating lanyard and waterproof case protecting an iPhone from loss and water damage.

Choosing a tough mobile device bag

iPhone photography bags can be good-looking, functional, and tough. Figure 8-17 shows my much loved iPhone Camera Bag by Waterfield Designs from San Francisco. This bag has been around the world a number of times and has the scars to prove it yet has always kept my iPhone safe.

The lower elastic straps are for a mini tripod or selfie stick, and the interior has dividers for extra items that you may want to pack for your next urban iPhone photography shoot. It comes in either leather or ballistic nylon.

FIGURE 8-17: The iPhone Camera Bag by Waterfield Designs.

Keeping your gear safe while traveling

One of the most popular iPhone cases is a wallet, such as Figure 8-18. While a wallet case is practical for day-to-day use, it's not an ideal option for when you're travelling. Even though you may be in a relatively safe destination, removing the temptation for thieves and pickpockets is an inexpensive insurance policy.

An iPhone itself has limited appeal for thieves as they know how well protected an iPhone is when the password is locked. An iPhone within a wallet, however, has much more appeal to a thief, so it's best to leave your wallet case at home when travelling.

Lighting Considerations

The beauty of travel, either for vacation or for adventure, is that you're pretty much guaranteed to encounter types of light that you're not used to in your own hometown. The following sections contain a sampling of types of light that you may encounter on your travels and corresponding iPhone photos so that you can mimic them to create your own travel photography gems!

Backlight

Backlight, or sometimes called *backlighting,* refers to light hitting your subject from behind. That would mean that your subject is between your camera and the sun or light source. Take a look at the Mexican papel picado colored flags in Figure 8-19. They appear to be glowing, don't they? And the mojigangas life-sized mannequin has an attractive rim of light around its head.

Backlighting has the wonderful ability to make translucent material, such as paper and foliage glow, and it also creates definition around people by creating a rim of light around their upper body.

Side light

Side light is fantastic for travel photography, especially in open spaces, such as the famous square in Riga, Latvia shown in Figure 8-20. Long shadows are cast when the sunlight is low, and you can make really good use of this light to capture people within their urban environments.

Don't worry that the beautiful buildings are a bit dark. The goal is less to document the famous landmarks, and rather to create artistic photos that capture the side light shadows cast by people walking through your composition.

Raking light

Raking light gets its name for the way in which the sun rakes along the surface of a flat object, such as the wall of a building. The light is at such a slight angle that most of the surface of the wall is in shadow. Any protrusions or texture on the wall will catch the sunlight, creating a very unique photograph similar to Figure 8-21.

To capture a photo similar to this Mexican exterior, watch for the time when the sunlight is low in the sky and is at such a slight angle to the building's surface that only flowers, door handles, or window shutters catch the light.

FIGURE 8-20:
Side lighting is often created by low sunlight shining between buildings.

FIGURE 8-21:
Raking light skims the surface of a wall, beautifully illuminating only objects or texture that protrude from the wall.

You only have about a two- or three-minute window of time to get this type of photo, as the rays of the low-lying sun move quickly.

Reflective light

Smooth or rain-soaked cobblestones have a stunning ability to reflect color. Don't forget to head out into town just after it rains, searching for colorful buildings that reflect onto the street. Figure 8-22 shows an example of a San Miguel de Allende, Mexico street that reflects color even when dry, due to the fact that the stones are so smooth and flat.

FIGURE 8-22:
Cobblestone streets can reflect the same color as the nearby buildings.

Diagonal light

Diagonal light is good for travel portraiture, especially when you ask your friend or family member to look in the direction of the light. Simply look for a great background that has light shining at approximately 45 degrees and place them within the scene based on the location of the light rays.

Figure 8-23 shows an example of a light ray that raked along a beautiful exterior, which made the perfect backdrop for a travel portrait session.

Silhouette light

The famous Cristo Rey statue in Guanajuato State in Mexico shows how you can use the sun to create artistic looking travel iPhone photos. When photographing famous landmarks, try to use the sun to create silhouettes of statues. Simply place your iPhone so that the sun is directly behind the statue, which will usually make the statue pitch black.

Figure 8-24 is an example of adding metaphor to a famous landmark. This statue of Christ is photographed hundreds of times every day. So how do you make your travel photo stand out from the crowd? Use artistic techniques such as silhouette lighting to add a sense of mystery and metaphor.

FIGURE 8-24:
Silhouette lighting
can add drama,
mystery, and
metaphor to your
travel photos.

Shadow light

Low-lying sunlight, such as sunset and sunrise, allows for stunning photo opportunities when travelling. Look for rays of light that shoot through structures and ask a family member to stand in the light. Try not to actually include them in the photo, just their shadow. This adds a sense of mystery and sometimes hilarity to your travel photos.

Figure 8-25 is an example where it appears that a friend's legs are elongated as if they were on massive stilts! You can have a lot of fun playing with shadows, especially if you have kids with you on your trip.

Magic hour light

Magic hour is a truly fantastic time of day to capture travel photos. Chapter 5 has a section dedicated to magic hour if you are interested in tips on how to make use of this unique type of light.

Figure 8-26 shows an example of a famous landmark scene in Jerusalem, Israel. The photo has a calming blueish color tone, and then when the sun was just about to peak through the clouds the atmosphere switched to a golden color tone, as shown in Figure 8-27.

FIGURE 8-25:
Look for rays of
light at sunrise or
sunset to allow
for unusual
shadow portraits.

FIGURE 8-26:
An example of
blue hour.

FIGURE 8-27:
An example of
golden hour.

If you have the time to wait in the same location, capture your desired travel scene in both blue and golden hours. Both of the photos will look pretty much the same compositionally, but the quality of light will make the photos truly unique.

Blue and yellow light

On the photographer's color wheel (not to be confused with the painter's color wheel), red and cyan are opposite colors, green and magenta are opposites, and blue and yellow are opposite colors. Out of these three opposing color combinations, blue and yellow are the most popular and visually appealing. This appeal may be due to the fact that all our lives we have witnessed blue and yellow together, such as the sun and sky, water and sun, golden farmer's fields plus blue sky, and many other blue and yellow combinations that we consider beautiful.

Figure 8-28 shows an example of a Japanese lantern that is illuminated by warm yellow light, and the interior of a shop that has blue light shining through the *shoji* paper screen window. The blue and yellow color combination of this composition provides a sense of harmony to the viewer.

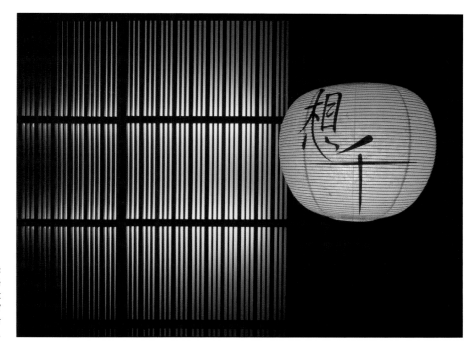

FIGURE 8-28:
Look for any type
of light that
exhibits the blue/
yellow color
combination.

The good news for your travel photography is that finding blue and yellow while on your journeys is easy. Artificial (electric) lights are often yellow-toned, so look for blue background behind the lights. Or simply make use of the naturally occurring yellow and orange warmth of the setting sun mixed with blue colors that you'll find while travelling.

Photography Tips for Your Next Trip

In the following sections, you discover a series of quick tips used by the top professional travel photographers. As you go through each tip and sample iPhone photo, keep a note of which techniques resonate with you and how you can plan to implement them on your next trip.

Practicing design-based photography

It's often tempting to photograph an entire beautiful building when travelling. That's fine, but to add a sense of fine art to your collection, try to focus on design-based photos that rely on form and angles. Figure 8-29 shows four photos taken of the same wall at different times of the day. These photos would be considered art photography more so than documentary photography. Place your photos together into a quadrant design using Instagram's Layout app for extra impact!

FIGURE 8-29: Photograph details that include angles and shadows for more of a fine art look and then combine them into a collage using apps like Layout.

Placing S-curves in your compositions

An S-curve is one of the oldest compositional technique in the history of art. Think of a painting of a garden with a path winding through it or a forest trail. These pathway scenes almost always have a curve to them, and rarely are straight-lined.

An S-curve is pleasing to the eye, and they're found often in nature and in urban environments. Figure 8-30 shows a mountain village scene in Nagano, Japan. The road exhibits a curve that leads the viewer's eye throughout the picture space. Keep in mind that the curve doesn't need to be in the exact shape of the letter S.

Framing your primary subject

Your travel photography should certainly contain normal documentary snapshots, but don't forget to add a sense of fine art to your images by using a compositional technique called *framing*.

The famous Parroquia in San Miguel de Allende, Mexico is photographed ad nauseum, so why not mix things up and hide most of the church by using a frame? Look for ways to visually enclose the iconic structure that you're photographing, such as well-positioned trees in Figure 8-31. By doing so, you will create a sense of mystery. Your viewer will be intrigued enough to ask to see more photos of that location.

Photographing exterior architecture twice

When travelling, you'll certainly encounter exterior buildings, shops, houses, and other buildings that look interesting to you. Use this general rule to successfully capture exterior façades, such as the Japanese shop front in Figure 8-32:

1. **Photograph the building façade perfectly straight on.**

2. **Then, photograph the building façade at a 45-degree angle as in Figure 8-33.**

These two angles are widely used by professional architectural photographers. It's rare that pros capture façades outside of these two angle options.

FIGURE 8-31:
By framing and partially hiding famous landmarks, you can create unique and mysterious travel photos.

FIGURE 8-32:
Completely straight-on is the most common way to photograph exteriors.

FIGURE 8-33:
Photographing at
a 45-degree angle
is another
popular way to
photograph
exteriors.

Including pattern photos of unusual scenes

While cobblestone streets may not be as unique to those who live in Europe or Latin America, for the rest of the world they certainly have charm for those who only experience pavement every day. When you see any type of scene that does not have a primary subject, such as hundreds of equally sized cobblestones, you can consider the scene an example of a pattern or texture photo.

Take a look at Figure 8-34. It has no unique main subject in the photo, because all of the cobblestones are the subject. You could consider this a pattern photo then, and by carefully composing so that the lines are even, you can create an intriguing frame-worthy travel photo. Just make sure that there is no object in your photo that would steal the attention away from the hundreds of other cobblestones.

Other texture or pattern photo examples are a brick wall, sand on the seashore, repeating tiles on an old church floor, and any scene where there is no visually distracting main subject that steals the attention from the rest of the picture.

FIGURE 8-34:
A pattern or texture photo doesn't contain a unique main subject, as each element in the photo is a similar size, shape, or tone.

Scheduling famous landmarks as early as possible

Have you ever planned to visit a highly Instagrammed famous location, hoping to get a photo when no one else is in your shot? With tourism on the rise worldwide, it's getting harder and harder to photograph without fellow tourists ruining your serene iPhone photo.

Figure 8-35 shows a very rare time when there was no one in the famous bamboo groves of Kyoto, Japan. The only reason this was possible was due to a 6 a.m. photo shoot start time! Yes, it's hard to wake up early when you've been photographing the night before, but your lack of sleep will be worth it to get the exact shot that you want.

Waiting for animals to move into the picture space

It's rare that you will be able to control the movements of an animal, so as a photographer you will just need a lot of patience. Take the swan in Figure 8-36, for example. It would have been better to have captured the swan when it was positioned a bit to the left, so that it was swimming into the picture space instead of swimming out of the picture space.

FIGURE 8-35:
If possible, plan
to arrive at iconic
locations as
soon as there is
light in the sky.

FIGURE 8-36:
When possible,
capture animals
moving so that
there is more
space in front
of them than
behind them.

You viewers will appreciate having the animal flow into your photo, as it's a more visually harmonious way to compose animals in motion.

Choosing your background first

Are you travelling with a group of friends or family members? Put your creative thinking hat on when deciding on group photo locations. If you are showing your travel photos publicly on social media, very few people will be interested in group photos with a blah-looking background.

Figure 8-37 is an example where I saw the location first and then gathered my friends for a fun group photo. Even go so far as place your friends so that their positioning is harmonious with the background. This is a great way for your social media friends and followers to stay engaged with your images, rather than flip quickly to the next picture.

FIGURE 8-37:
Find your backgrounds first and then add your friends and family members second.

Matching color when possible

For lack of a better term, *matching color* simply means that you wait until another person, animal, car, or other moving object enters your composition that has the same color. This technique is rarely practiced because it involves a lot of waiting.

Take Figure 8-38, for example. I saw the classic green VW Beetle and also knew that San Miguel de Allende taxis are also painted the same green color. So, with a relatively easy five-minute wait, crouched in position, the magic happened when the taxi drove straight into the composition.

Including national text and fonts in your photos

It won't matter that most of your viewers won't be able to read the letters of the foreign language that you just photographed on your overseas trip. The main priority, however, is that you successfully added a *sense of place* for the sake of your viewer.

While your viewers may not know Thai script as in Figure 8-39, they may assume that the script looks like a South-East Asian language. Without any description to tell them what the language is, they at least can place the photo in a rough geographic area.

Composing with equidistance

The Corinth canal in Greece is a stunning location for iPhone photos and videos. When you encounter a scene like this canal, you will see that location is symmetrical. The left side is pretty much the same as the right side, with the canal in the dead-center.

Usually when you see a symmetrical scene, it's best to compose your image using *equidistance*. When used as a photographic term, equidistance simply means that the left side distance is equivalent to the right-side distance. Take a look at Figure 8-40. The canal is placed perfectly centered so that the cliffs have the same distance measurements on either side of the canal.

Tightening the view of iconic buildings

When travelling, it's often advantageous to try every trick in the book to take your photos from documentary snapshots to fine art travel photos. One way to do this is to look at a famous landmark and choose a detail to capture rather than showing the whole structure.

FIGURE 8-40:
When your subject exhibits symmetry, make sure that the left side and the right side have the same distance measurements within your composition.

The Leaning Tower of Pisa is a great example. This location is one of the most photographed in the world, so how can your photo stand out from the crowd? Try to tighten your view of the tower, or whatever you're photographing, so that you are creating a detail photo. Throw in your favorite black-and-white filter, and you just created a frame-worthy fine art wall-hanging, similar to Figure 8-41.

FIGURE 8-41:
Iconic structures can be interpreted just as effectively as detail shots, where you choose your iPhone's telephoto lens or you zoom in.

Composing family members looking into the frame

Everybody wants to look good when being photographed during vacation or travelling. So, the next time that you photograph your friend or family member at that stunning Greek island beach, ask him or her to look into the picture space. This simply means that there will be far more space in front of the person than behind, as in Figure 8-42.

FIGURE 8-42: Have your model to the side of your frame, where they are looking into the picture space instead of looking out of the picture.

Reviewing your favorite establishments

Did you just enjoy the best chocolate of your life while in Europe? Or maybe an unbeatable gordita while in Mexico? If you had a really positive experience at a local business while travelling, take a moment to give that establishment a positive review on Trip Advisor, Google, Facebook, Yelp, and any other review site. Local establishments can greatly benefit by your reviews, which allows them to provide for their families and continue to produce great products and services.

When I visit Jerusalem, I can't get enough of Arabic coffee served in the traditional way, as in Figure 8-43. This café near the Western Wall is my go-to both in the morning and midday. After that blast of delicious caffeine, I'm good to go for a lot more iPhone photographs!

FIGURE 8-43:
Help local establishments by posting positive reviews when you are travelling.

IN THIS CHAPTER

» Choosing shaped plates for still life arrangements

» Photographing with mixed light

» Creating a seamless background using Bristol board

» Using opaque paper as a background

» Choosing to photograph in both color and black and white

» Adding negative space for text

Chapter **9**

Creating Still Life and Product Photography on the Cheap

This chapter is all about photographing objects to be used either for art or commerce. Do you have or plan to have an online store for your products? Do you want to create fine art photographic prints to sell online? If so, this chapter is for you.

Maybe you don't really have any aspirations to photograph commercially. No problem! Please read this chapter anyway, as it has some helpful tips and tricks that apply to other photographic genres as well.

Camera Considerations

A *still life photograph* is usually an inanimate object that is somewhat small, whereby the photographer aims to capture the object in an artistic manner. Still life photos are often created to be framed and presented at galleries, or hanging on walls in people's homes.

Still life photos can also be used commercially. Think of a product photo, such as a handmade mug that a potter photographed for online sales purposes.

Still life and product photography doesn't really have any unique camera considerations that you need to know prior to capturing your first image. The main technique that you'll probably want to make use of, however, is being able to adjust exposure. The word *exposure* simply means how bright or how dark your photo is when you take a photo, or the brightness levels that you can adjust when editing your photo.

To be able to make your photo brighter or darker prior to snapping the photo (called *exposure compensation*), follow these simple steps:

1. **Compose your image so that your subject is placed in a way that you feel looks good.**

2. **On your screen, press and hold your finger over your still life subject.**

3. **When your subject has a yellow box around it, scroll your finger up for a brighter look.**

4. **Scroll your finger down the screen for a darker look.**

Chapter 7 has a visual instruction on exposure compensation.

Gear Considerations

Each photographic genre requires at least one unique item of gear or prop. Still life and product photographs are more about props than extra photographic gear. In this section, you discover some props that can help you create stunning still life iPhone photographs.

REMEMBER

Tripods are not mandatory, especially when photographing with plenty of window light, although they do afford the photographer a better quality image when the light is a bit lower than normal.

Purchasing backgrounds for flat-lay still life photos

Are you good at flower arranging, or at least would like to learn more about that artform? Why not frame up your flowers or any groupings of objects with a shaped plate? Figure 9-1's stunning succulent arrangement found in San Miguel de Allende's *Fabrica la Aurora* is a great example of a framed arrangement. A simple but effective heart-shaped plate holds a visually delightful collection of succulents.

When photographing with a shaped plate, keep these tips in mind:

>> Create one blast of color to draw your viewer's attention (red succulent in the midst of green succulents).

>> Choose a shadow area or an overcast day, as harsh sunlight is tricky to photograph successfully.

>> Photograph from an aerial perspective, meaning straight down.

>> Try to position yourself so that your shadow isn't cast onto your photo.

Choosing the appropriate background for your product

When creating still life photos for either artistic or commercial purposes, always ask yourself if your choice of background complements your subject. Take a look at Figure 9-2. The aged boards are a perfect choice as a background for the collection of historic woodworking tools.

FIGURE 9-2:
Choose backgrounds that complement (or at least don't distract from) the main subject.

TIP

If your next thought is "but I don't feel confident in knowing if my background complements by subject," don't worry! This common concern is one that can easily be allayed. The only thing that you need to judge is whether the background visually competes with the subject matter for your viewer's attention. If the background isn't as interesting as your subject, you most likely chose correctly.

The exception to this general background rule is when you're purposefully trying to shock your viewer. In that case, you'll want to choose a background that clashes with your main subject. While this practice is rare, you should at least know about it in case your goal is to create a sense of tension in your still life photo.

Using clear glass as a background

The famous Mexican chocolate shop JOHFREJ created a clever way to present its delicious hot chocolate to its customers. As in Figure 9-3, it placed cocoa beans on top of a rimmed table and then a circular plate of glass laid over the beans. This arrangement presented a delightful way to show off its product.

FIGURE 9-3: A plate of glass over your smaller product samples looks fantastic as a background.

You can do the same to create a unique background for you still life photos. Simply place smallish objects that are related to your primary still life product, cover them with a sheet of glass, and then create your still life product or art photos.

TIP

Be careful to avoid reflections that often accompany photos that include glass. Experiment with the position and the angle in which you photograph, and you'll eventually find an angle that avoids reflections. Try to illuminate your still life with window light only, avoiding overhead electric lights.

Floating flowers in water

Another gem from Mexico's *Fabrica la Aurora* art galleries, Figure 9-4 shows a floating display of flowers within a large plant pot. Are you passionate about photographing flowers? This style of still life photography works wonderfully with water. Simply find an artistic looking large plant pot and let your favorite flowers float on the surface.

FIGURE 9-4:
Use water as a background for your flower still life photos.

Purchasing Bristol board for interior product photography

Figure 9-5 shows *Bristol board*, which is a poster-sized sheet of thick paper similar to card stock. It's often used by DIY photo studio enthusiasts as well as many professional studio photographers who like how inexpensive and versatile the paper is.

Your local art supply or dollar store will most likely have Bristol board in multiple colors. Choose white for most still life backgrounds, but also buy other colors. In the upcoming "Lighting Considerations" section, you can see how a sheet of Bristol board is used for a clean and beautiful white background for any small product.

Photographing still life photos in a greenhouse

This older iPhone 6 Plus photo in Figure 9-6 holds up remarkably well considering that the 6 Plus was not nearly as advanced as recent model iPhones. One of the reasons that the photo looks so soft and pleasing is because it was photographed within a greenhouse.

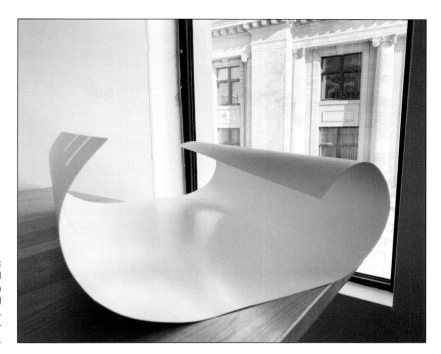

FIGURE 9-5:
Bristol board
creates an
edge-less and
smooth back-
ground for your
products.

FIGURE 9-6:
Greenhouses
often have
opaque glass that
soften the light
falling on plants
and flowers.

Greenhouses often have sections where the glass above or on the sides is actually opaque instead of perfectly clear. This opaque glass will soften all of your still life plant and flower photography, even with harsh noonday light. The word *opaque* simply means that light can seep through the material, but the material is not perfectly see-through.

Adding opaque paper to windows for unique backgrounds

Windows make excellent backgrounds for your product or still life, but the brightness of the background window light can often be overpowering. Try covering your window in *vellum paper* or any other opaque material.

Figure 9-7 is a good example of a textured window covering made of Japanese rice paper. The paper is also textured using paint, which allows for a calming and beautiful background for the still life subject. Most art supply stores carry various vellum or opaque papers that you can use as window coverings.

FIGURE 9-7: You can use opaque and textured paper attached to windows as still life backgrounds.

If you decided on a textured opaque paper, try to judge whether the design on the paper complements your still life subject matter. The background shouldn't seem visually jarring or out-of-place with your subject.

Lighting Considerations

Still life photos rely heavily on artistic lighting, which is what this section is all about. Think of artistic lighting as a way to illuminate your still life in a way that goes far beyond a normal camera flash illumination. Your goal is to create artwork that is worthy of framing and hanging on your wall!

Photographing your product indoors

In the preceding section, you discover that Bristol board is a must-have piece of home-studio gear. Take a look at Figures 9-8 and 9-9 to see why. In Figure 9-8, you can see the still life product, which is a handmade pottery mug that needed to be photographed for a pottery sales website. In Figure 9-9, you see the finished product, an iPhone 11 Pro photo suitable for e-commerce websites or a potter's portfolio.

FIGURE 9-8:
Bristol board taped to a windowsill provides a seamless backdrop for product photography.

FIGURE 9-9:
The finished
photo with the
white material in
the background
being a curved
sheet of Bristol
board.

TECHNICAL STUFF

A bit of studio photography lingo trivia: The curved effect of the Bristol board that you see in Figure 9-8 is called a *sweep*, or sometimes a *seamless*. These two terms reflect the fact that you won't see any harsh edges behind your product.

Follow these steps to create a similar product photo that uses a seamless white Bristol board as a background.

1. **Choose either a north-facing window or an overcast day for your product still life photos.**

2. **Tape a white Bristol board onto your windowsill to provide a seamless sweep background.**

3. **Place your product or artistic still life onto the Bristol board.**

WARNING

4. **Use your iPhone's most telephoto lens.**

   Don't use your widest-angle lens.

5. **Lighten up the product by pressing the screen and holding on the subject and then swiping upward for more brightness.**

6. **Take the photo.**

   If you feel the product is too bright or too dark, re-adjust the exposure and take the photo again.

To find out how to make your photo brighter or darker using the screen press and hold method, refer to Chapter 7.

Using side light

If your house has horizontal morning or evening sun rays shooting through your windows, make use of that gorgeous side lighting by placing a still life object within the light ray. Find an appropriate stand to keep your still life stable and move it around until you like the composition, similar to the example in Figure 9-10.

FIGURE 9-10:
Side lighting inside houses often come from morning or evening sunlight shining through windows.

REMEMBER

Don't forget that you may need to make your photo a bit darker than usual if you find that your still life subject is far too bright. This often happens when your still life subject is light in tone and your background is a bit dark.

Using backlight

Backlighting can best be described as a strong light source shining through an opaque material. Similar to the previously mentioned Japanese rice paper covering a window, backlighting is effective with foliage or paper products.

Figure 9-11 shows a Japanese paper umbrella where the paper is opaque enough to allow warm light to pass through. And by photographing the Figure 9-12 green foliage from the underside on a sunny day, you can replicate the fern leaf photo on the right side of the figure.

FIGURE 9-11:
Paper products
are a perfect
opaque material
for back-lit still
life photos.

FIGURE 9-12:
When the sun
shines on the top
surface of a leaf,
foliage has a
wonderful glow
when you
photograph
from below.

Using harsh overhead light

Midday direct overhead sunlight is usually harsh and unforgiving for photographs. And that time of day is especially difficult to photograph flowers! However, Figure 9-13 demonstrates an exception. It's a photo from Hotel Santa Monica in San Miguel de Allende, Mexico, where the flower still life arrangement looks fantastic even though it is illuminated by the harshest overhead light possible.

FIGURE 9-13: A flower arrangement still life scene illuminated by harsh, overhead midday sunlight.

As long as you move backwards and photograph your midday flower arrangements as a wide scene with a lot of the surrounding area included, you should be able to get away with the harsh lighting. Because the blue sky was included in the composition, plus the hotel and fountain, our attention is not distracted by the small harsh light reflections that are actually on each flower petal. Because you are seeing these flowers from a distance, any lighting imperfections or distractions are not even noticed.

Using doorway light

Although most of the examples in this chapter are smallish still life products or objects, you can create larger objects like life sized papier mâché figures. You certainly can't use a single sheet of white Bristol board for large objects.

Take a look at Figure 9-14, which is a papier mâché figure placed in the doorway of a San Miguel de Allende restaurant called Don Taco Tequila. The restaurant successfully used this large still life character as a means of attracting attention. The character enriches the restaurant both artistically and commercially. But what is the best way to photograph life-size objects such as this papier mâché man?

FIGURE 9-14:
Doorway light works perfectly for life-size still life subjects.

By placing your large object in an exterior doorway, you can light the object perfectly, and usually your background will become very dark. This effect is because the outside streetlight is almost always brighter than the artificial light in shops, bars, and restaurants. This contrast of light is a good thing, as the dark or black background really pushes all visual attention on your still life. When you take your photo, feel free to include the doorway or go tighter to avoid the doorway altogether.

Photographing with mixed lighting

When your still life photo is equally illuminated with window light and your interior electric lightbulbs, one side of your still life subject will have a blue sheen, and the other side will have a warmish orange/yellow tone.

Take a look at Figure 9-15, which shows a still life image taken in the excellent Illuseum tea house in Riga, Latvia. The window light cast a bluish color on the left of the tea pot, and the overhead electric lights reflected warm tones.

Bluish Window Light

Yellow Lightbulb Light

FIGURE 9-15: Window light casts cool color tones, and lightbulbs (usually) cast warm color tones.

This mixed lighting scenario can either be good or bad, depending on your still life subject matter and, of course, what you prefer. If you feel that you really just need one color tone for your still life, try turning off all your interior house lights to rely solely on window light.

Adding shadows to your still life photos

Plant or flower still life photos are incredibly popular as wall art, and you can take the fine art vibe even further by taking or converting your photo to black and white. If you also include a shadow in your still life, such as Figure 9-16, you will have added a sense of metaphor or poetry to your still life image.

FIGURE 9-16: Add metaphor and poetry to your still life compositions by including shadows.

Photographing throughout the day

You may have products that need to be photographed for advertising purposes. Take a look at the Mexican cross of Figure 9-17, which was photographed in the morning. When you locate the perfect background for your product photography, make sure that you make use of changing light throughout the day. For example, the photograph in Figure 9-18 was taken in the late afternoon. The differences in light throughout the day offer varied background options for your subject matter.

Daytime photography can benefit from dramatic light rays shining through windows, and evening light can provide a softer, more welcoming appearance for your product photos.

FIGURE 9-17:
Make use of
morning light for
your product or
still life.

FIGURE 9-18:
With your
product in the
same location,
photograph it in
the very different
light of afternoon
or evening.

Creating Beautiful Still Life Photos

If you have a good understanding of how to light your still life product, you are ready for a few pro tips to help you master the genre. In the following sections, I offer still life and product photography tips for you to practice. With each day of photography, you will see yourself get better at both the technical and the creative side of still life photography.

Composing symmetrical photos properly

While this next tip may sound overly simplistic and obvious, it's remarkable how many people don't care to balance their compositions symmetrically. Take a look at Figure 9-19 of an artist's studio in the famous Fabrica la Aurora art complex in Mexico. Because the doorway is symmetrical, we can safely ignore the Rule of Thirds. Place your still life subject, in this case the potted cactus plant, dead-center in the frame.

FIGURE 9-19:
With symmetrical scenes, it's often best to avoid the Rule of Thirds and compose your still life subject dead-centered.

The Rule of Thirds is a fantastic tool for nonsymmetrical scenes, but often not the best looking when the background is perfectly symmetrical. See Chapter 5 for what the Rule of Thirds is and how you can apply it to most of your photos.

Arranging foliage to catch the setting sun

If your chosen still life subject matter are live plants or flowers from a field or forest, make use of the setting sun to provide backlight. The sun will hit the back of the foliage, which creates a beautiful warm glow, as in Figure 9-20.

FIGURE 9-20: Backlit foliage glows, which makes for beautiful still life nature photos.

If you're averse to picking the foliage, you can still catch the sunlight by simply by moving the stem of the plant so that it sticks up above the rest of the foliage. If you have a friend with you, this process of repositioning the fern will be much easier.

Following the equidistance principle

While not a deal-breaker, when composing a still life scene, such as these Japanese books in Figure 9-21, follow the principle of *equidistance*. Equidistance means that the most important part of your subject should have a surrounding space that is equivalent on the opposing sides.

FIGURE 9-21:
Equidistance
requires equal
empty or white
space on either
side of the
still life object.

Take a look at the horizontal arrows in Figure 9-21. The white-space distance between the top corners of the books is pretty much equal. Similarly, the vertical arrows show equidistance vertically.

REMEMBER

Don't feel that you need to slavishly follow the principle of equidistance. It's only a guide or suggestion that you can safely ignore as you like. Remember, it's always best to know the rules first, and then you can break them.

Creating both color and black-and-white versions

Choosing one of the three black-and-white filters for your still life photo has a lot of value, as black-and-white still life images traditionally tend to be considered more artistic. That doesn't have to be true necessarily, as, of course, art can and should be in color. So then, why not add value to your collection by taking both a color and a black-and-white version of your photo, as in Figure 9-22?

TIP

You can either take a photo in black and white and then color or just take one photo in color and then convert it to black and white later within your iPhone's Photos app.

FIGURE 9-22:
Having both a
color and
black-and-white
version of your
photo extends
your photo's
usability and
value.

Adding negative space to be used for text

The term *negative space* can loosely be described as empty, detail-less space that surrounds the subject matter. In the case of Figure 9-23, the red wall is a type of negative space. The reason why you'd want to include more empty space than usual is to extend the future usability of your photos. This photo could be used as a cover photo of a magazine, a vertical business card, a lovely postcard, or any other printed material that requires both a photo and text overlaid on that photo.

FIGURE 9-23:
Negative space
in a photo
composition
allows for space
for text.

Chapter **10**

Taking It to the Streets: Photographing Strangers

Photographing strangers in urban environments is a controversial topic, as issues such as privacy and consent are legitimate factors that should shape your decision-making process. Should you photograph those people walking down the street? Or would that infringe on their privacy?

I deal with these ethical questions in this chapter, as well as offer tips and techniques for creating the best possible street photos using the most inobtrusive means possible.

Camera Considerations

Street photography as a genre has a rich history. In fact, the first known photograph that showed a person on the street was by Louis Daguerre in 1838. Since then, the art of street photography has done nothing but increase in historical value and viewer fascination. In this section, you discover ways to get your iPhone's camera ready to capture your own slice of urban life.

Choosing black and white for most photos

The history of street photography is largely a record of the urban world presented in black and white. Either by using black and white film, or converting color photos to black and white, past and current street photographers tend to prefer a monochromatic image. But there are many exceptions! You'll often encounter a street photo similar to Figure 10-1, where it's the green color that makes the photo. When the photo is digitally converted to black and white as in Figure 10-2, the image loses a sense of uniqueness.

FIGURE 10-1:
Keep street photography in color when the color is considered an important aspect of the photo.

REMEMBER

Another factor to consider regarding your choice of color or black and white is simply taste. Because the photo is your artwork, always present it the way that you want to show it, not the way that you feel other people would want you to present it.

To photograph in black and white, choose either a Mono, Silvertone, or Noir camera filter. (To find out how to access these filters, refer to Chapter 2.) Don't be afraid to photograph using a filter within your normal iPhone camera app. Even though it looks like you just took a black-and-white photo, the original color image is saved within the image file. This means that you can access the color version anytime in the future within the iOS Photos app.

You can also create black-and-white photos from any of your color photos by using your iPhone's editing tools. Chapter 11 goes into editing techniques in greater detail.

Cropping best practices

When creating street photos, you will no doubt encounter situations where the main part of your photo is excellent, but something on the edges of the composition is distracting. If so, simply crop your photo! Yes, feel free to crop your image to only have the most important parts visible. *Cropping* means that you cut out part of your image from either one or up to four sides of your image.

In Figure 10-3, at the top left of the photo are distracting awnings, so with a simple crop from left to right as in Figure 10-4, the photo was made more clean-looking.

Chapter 11 explains cropping options that can really empower your photo to new levels.

FIGURE 10-3:
An awning in the
top left of the
photo is slightly
distracting.

FIGURE 10-4:
Cropping out
distracting parts
of your photo can
add visual
strength to your
street images.

Placing more importance on drama instead of sharpness

Street photography gets a pass when it comes to technically sharp images. There is usually more importance on a photo's soul than being technically sharp and composed. But what is *soul,* and how do you define such a metaphysical characteristic?

Take a look at Figure 10-5. This iPhone photo is certainly not the sharpest, but it presents to the viewer a certain sense of loneliness or introspection. Does this photo tell a story? Does it elicit a particular emotional response from the viewer? If so, you could arguably say that this photo has soul. Technical perfection usually takes a back seat to a sense of emotion within the street photography genre.

FIGURE 10-5: Street photography relies less on technical excellence and more on emotion and drama.

Using background blur to maintain privacy

The ability to blur the background used to be the domain of DSLR cameras, but now all late model iPhones can produce such an effect. Take a look at Figure 10-6, which shows a model on a subway train advertisement, with blurred real people on the train. If you want to maintain anonymity but still create a dynamic urban street photo, why not focus on fake people and let the real people behind fall into a pleasing background blur?

In Portrait mode, you can long-press any two-dimensional face or even an object that isn't human. If you're not too tight for time, give this technique a try. Do a Portrait mode photo on anything that is in the foreground, and the people in the background will be visible but not sharply defined.

FIGURE 10-6:
In Portrait mode you can focus on almost anything, which will cause the background to be blurred.

Photographing with Burst mode for perfect timing

Street photography is similar in some respects to sports photography, in that you often need to act quickly. Not only are fast reflexes an asset, you also need to have perfect timing where the subject is artistically placed within the background.

Take a look at Figure 10-7, for example. I saw the chalk square on the wall and a young man walking down the street. Assuming that his head would enter the background chalk square, Burst mode's rapid fire of photos guaranteed that at least one of the photos would work perfectly.

Many of the tips in this chapter give you both technical tips and pointers on how to photograph people in a way that protects their identity. If you're photographing a scene similar to Figure 10-7, all you need to do is wait until the person slightly passes by the front of your iPhone and then start the Burst mode. This technique captures only his or her side profile without disclosing too many facial features.

FIGURE 10-7:
Use Burst mode
when you need
your subject to be
perfectly placed
within a specific
background.

Gear Considerations

When it comes to extra gear purchasing needs, street photography is notoriously inexpensive. In fact, the less gear you have, the better, as the last thing you want while creating urban street scenes is to lug around expensive and heavy photo gear. Keep it small and light!

Using waterproof cases for rainy days

Chapter 8 is all about travel photography, and in it is some specific suggestions on water and weatherproof cases for your iPhone. In street photography, you'll also want to have protection from the elements because sometimes the very best street photos are taken in bad weather.

Figure 10-8 is a photo taken from my annual photo workshop in Italy, where the main instruction was how to successfully photograph during rainstorms. One of the best aspects of rainy street photography is all of the umbrellas that suddenly pop up!

If you have an iPhone from any generation earlier than the 7 series, you'll need to order a waterproof case if you plan to photograph in heavy rain. If you have an iPhone 7 series model or later, your phone has a water resistance rating that will allow you to photograph in the rain without a waterproof case.

Even though late model iPhones have an impressive water resistance rating, you'd be forgiven for playing it safe. If you have the budget for extra water resistance gear, then by all means make use of a specialized case. If you want to rely on your iPhone's water-resistant body, just make sure you dry off your iPhone according to Apple's suggestions that you can find on its website.

Choosing other stability options besides tripods

It's rare that street photographers tote around a tripod. Not only is a tripod slow to set up, a tripod also just doesn't fit in to the general ethos of street photography. In street photography, you're allowing the urban environment to imprint itself on you. A wonderful moment can come and go within seconds, so you need to always be walking and always be watching. A tripod will remove a degree of spontaneity to your urban photo session.

In saying all that, however, there are times when it's just too dark to get a decent street photo using an iPhone. If you're using any iPhone older than the 11 series, feel free to stabilize your iPhone on anything that is solid and still.

Figure 10-9 is a good example of an iPhone 6 Plus photo that needed a bit of stability help. During another one of my photo workshops, this one held in Tokyo, the goal was to practice photographing the giant eye with people walking past the wonderfully bizarre art installation. Because the workshop participants were not using tripods, they rested their iPhones on a flat-topped railing. This stability of being both handheld and on a flat stable surface allowed the eyeball to be sharp, and the woman to be artistically blurred due to motion.

FIGURE 10-9:
In very dark environments, use a stable platform to rest your iPhone on for better image quality.

Interestingly, the iPhone 11 series has a feature called Night mode that turns on automatically when your scene is very dark. Night mode is quite impressive and works well in environments that previously needed tripods or a stable platform.

Lighting Considerations

Street photography is less about gear and more about light. This section helps you master the light that falls into urban spaces, which gives your street photos a drama-filled fine art appearance.

Waiting for people to walk into a ray of light

You can create stunning street photos within your own urban environment simply by looking for strong rays of light that shoot between buildings. Take a look at Figure 10-10 as an example and try the following steps to create a similar photo.

FIGURE 10-10:
Wait for people to walk through shafts of light.

1. **Find a street scene with a ray of light shining between buildings.**

2. **Compose your photo that shows both the ray of light and the surrounding streetscape.**

3. **Focus on the ray of light by long-pressing on the screen with your finger.**

4. **When you see a yellow square appear on your screen, scroll downward to make your photo darker.**

5. **Now wait for someone to walk into the ray of light and take the photo.**

Allowing shadows to work as metaphors

Take a look at Figure 10-11 and ask yourself if any storyline is present in the picture. How about this one, for example: "The teenager feels the heavy weight of becoming an adult. His younger childhood self walks with him, signified by the shadow. The child also feels a sense of loss, as he realizes that his older self is losing the innocence of being young."

FIGURE 10-11: Look for shadows, which often add a poetic or metaphoric element to your street photos.

How's that for being prosaic! I'm a photographer and obviously not a poet.

Regardless of how well-crafted your storyline is, a good street photo tells a story or offers the viewer ample opportunity for interpretation. Metaphors are present in street photography, and you can capture these literary dynamics in your urban photos as well.

Blurring people by photographing at dusk

The term *motion-blur,* when used in its photographic meaning, refers to a moving object that is slightly blurred due to either a slower shutter speed, fast movement, or a combination of both. Motion blur has been evident and widely used since the very first photograph. While it's true that mobile device cameras, such as iPhones, have a harder time creating perfect motion blur, you can increase your chances simply by photographing when the light is low.

Figure 10-12 is an example of iPhone motion blur where the man has a pleasing degree of unsharpness, and everything else (including the stopped tram) is sharp. There were no special tricks to this Riga, Latvia street photo, simply a steady hand holding the iPhone and enough darkness at dusk to render the man blurred.

Maintaining anonymity by using backlight

An effective way to avoid seeing faces yet maintaining a high degree of artfulness is to photograph people's backs when the light is shining on their faces. This is called backlight, and when the light is strong, it can create very dramatic street images.

Figure 10-13 shows an example of a Jerusalem resident going home after getting groceries. This photo is successful in the sense that there is no lack of drama, even though we can't identify the person. Street photography can work just as well for those who are apprehensive about photographing people without permission.

Capturing mannequins with window reflections

Did you know that nonliving humans are just as valid a street photography subject as real people? Look around for interesting ways to capture mannequins, especially making use of window reflections similar to Figure 10-14.

WARNING

Keep in mind that higher-end shops may have a copyright on their professionally designed window displays, so you may be limited as to what you can do with the photographs commercially. However, creating mannequin street photography just for the fun of it is payment enough.

Photographing only a person's shadow for extra mystery

Used heavily in film noir movies of the '40s and '50s, the depiction of a person's shadow usually elicits a strong emotional reaction in the viewer. What does the person look like? We have no idea. What are his or her motives? Is the person dangerous? These thoughts often come to mind when only the shadow of a person is present.

In Figure 10-15, you do see the person's legs, but his identity and intent is a mystery. And what is he holding in his hand? It's hard to tell.

FIGURE 10-14:
Photographing
mannequins at
dusk allows for
interesting
reflections
in the glass.

FIGURE 10-15:
Shadow
photography
in urban
environments
adds tension to
your scene.

TIP

Make use of shadows to create a sense of unease in your street photos. You will both have a very dramatic image and also not be concerned about being overly obtrusive.

Raking light for textured backgrounds

A lot of street photography makes use of a term called the *fishing technique*. In this technique, you find a cool-looking background, and then you wait until the fish grabs the bait. In Figure 10-16, I saw the wonderfully textured wall and waited for someone interesting to walk into the composition.

FIGURE 10-16: Raking light means that the sun is at a very slight angle to the wall, which shows off texture.

But the fishing technique doesn't always work, and it can get boring fast. To maintain the interest level in your viewers, look for a wall that exhibits texture. Raking light is a term that describes a wall or any non-smooth surface whereby the slight angle of the sun *rakes along* the surface, showing off the wall's texture.

With this type of light, you can maintain an interesting background that visually supports the main subject, which is the person.

Photography Tips for Your Next Day (or Night) on the Town

As with most photography genres, street photography has well established best practices. This section is jam-packed with tips, techniques, and also the philosophy or ethical parameters of photographing people whom you don't know.

Finding your background first

Many professional street photographers rely on finding a cool background first and then waiting for the right people to walk into their frame. This technique is effective for creating fine art street photography, but it comes with a catch: You need to be incredibly patient! Take a look at Figure 10-17 of a Tokyo mall escalator scene, which required me about 5 minutes of waiting until the people's position in the frame looked good.

FIGURE 10-17: You will get better results by not feeling rushed when waiting for people to walk into your chosen background.

TIP

Street photography is a solo sport. It's hard to wait around for the right people to enter your frame if you're on a group tour or with friends who want to keep moving to the next destination.

To avoid the inevitable recipe for frustration that comes with travelling with non-street photographers, schedule your street photography sessions when you can be alone. By doing so, you will be able to wait at one single location for as long as you need to get the shot that you like.

Choosing an aerial perspective

For those who prefer not to have people's faces visible or recognizable, train yourself to photograph from alternate vantage points, such as an aerial perspective. Go to second floor windows when possible, and photograph downward.

Figure 10-18 is a good example of an Italian cyclist photographed from my hotel room window. It was an easy photograph to take, and because no faces were visible, the photo could be sold commercially.

FIGURE 10-18:
Photograph from an aerial perspective to retain both anonymity and artistry.

Being culturally sensitive

Figure 10-19 is a photo of a woman purchasing bread in Jerusalem. As I had no intention of showing her face for culturally appropriate reasons, this vantage point both retains privacy and also demonstrates a slice of life in the streets of

Jerusalem's Old City. By viewing the photo, we can imagine the wonderful smell of the freshly baked bread and how buying that bread could be a daily ritual for the residents of the Old City.

FIGURE 10-19:
Understand
culturally
appropriate
parameters
before you start
photographing.

What follows is a non-exhaustive list of parameters or considerations that will hopefully help you in deciding what is appropriate for street photography and what you may be best to walk away from:

>> Know the local laws before you start photographing. Does the country or municipality that you're photographing in legally allow for street photography? If not, can you photograph people but just not show recognizable features?

>> When you are photographing people within their urban environment, are you conscious of not making them look foolish or embarrassing? Unless you are a photojournalist who is covering a specific story, it's best to show people in either a neutral or empowering light.

>> Street photography is almost always unplanned, so it's rare that you'd ask someone's permission and then take the photo. But always feel free to show the person the photo that you just took after the fact, and offer to delete it if they are uncomfortable with the shot.

>> When you're in cities that have strong political or religious views, such as in Figure 10-19, always do your research to understand what the ethical parameters should be for photographing people on the streets. You should do this even if the country has no laws against street photography.

>> Street musicians and buskers deserve tips, so if you photograph people who are offering music or are performing, show them some appreciation by offering them a donation.

>> If you're planning to photograph within a conflict zone, you'll probably be working within photojournalistic parameters rather than street photography parameters. *Photojournalism* is a different photographic genre than street photography and has very different industry-specific rules and norms. Photojournalism is not within the scope of this book, but it's a worthwhile genre for you to study. A *photojournalist* is a photographer who has training in journalistic writing, and whose photos usually support a written piece of news destined for publishing in print or web.

Maintaining a sense of lightness and humor

Does the world get a bit too serious and heavy at times? Most likely, your answer is an overwhelming *yes*. To counter that sentiment, always be on the lookout for lighthearted, fun, and encouraging street photography when you're out with your iPhone. All of us need to smile and laugh each day to stay healthy, and what better way to do this than through the art of street photography?

Figure 10-20 shows the cardboard cut-outs of a popular musical group in Japan and a fan taking a selfie with the group members in the background. There is no need to think that street photography must always be dramatic or philosophically deep. Something as simple as a fan getting a photo with her favorite musical group is just as worthy to be considered a street photograph.

One quick note on the ethics of having faces visible within countries that do not have laws against street photography. Ask yourself whether the person in your photo would feel ridiculed or embarrassed. If the answer is no, then also ask yourself if the photo was taken in a public place with people all around. Busy public places, such as Tokyo station, have very different ethical parameters than a back alley with no one around except a single person.

FIGURE 10-20:
Look for humor in the streets, which will balance out the sometimes serious or heavy side of urban life.

Choosing the best stride

TIP

When people walk past your iPhone, try using Burst mode so that you can choose the best stride later on when you're reviewing your photos. Often, your street photo can be ruined by a silly looking stride, simply because the person's two legs were in a split-second awkward position. To avoid this problem, take many photos using Burst mode, and then you'll have plenty of great looking variations to choose from.

Figure 10-21 is an example of the perfect stride, chosen from six other Burst photos that actually didn't look natural.

Showing the urban environment using a wide lens

Professional street photographers usually limit themselves to just one lens, which is called a *35mm prime*. You can purchase this type of lens for your DSLR or mirrorless camera, and it offers the street photographer a perfect balance between wide angle views and the view that the human eye sees. These types of lenses also do not zoom, which means that you, as the photographer, have to physically move closer to the subject or farther away, instead of relying on zooming the lens.

FIGURE 10-21:
Use Burst mode
for street photos
when people are
walking past you
and then choose
the photo with
the best-looking
stride.

Take a look at Figure 10-22, which shows a typical lens viewing angle that is similar to a 35mm prime lens for larger DSLR cameras. One immediate aspect of the photo that you may see is that the main subject, the man, is quite small in the photo. If he is the primary subject, shouldn't he be much more prominent in the image? Not necessarily! Street photography presents a sense of scale when the person is actually quite small.

TIP

To mimic the look of a street photographer's 35mm prime lens, try to avoid your iPhone's telephoto lens and also avoid digitally zooming in using the pinch-to-zoom technique. Some iPhone models have a telephoto option, and it's tempting to use that lens to visually bring your subject closer and more prominent in the photo. However wider angle views tend to be a better choice for street photography to show your viewer what the urban environment actually looks like.

Composing with a sense of direction

Take a look at Figure 10-23 and ask yourself if there is a sense of direction in the photo. If so, what is the direction? In this image, the visual flow of the photo is clearly from right to left. The chef and the VW Beetle are both heading in the same direction. This uniformity of motion provides a sense of visual harmony even though in reality the VW is stationary.

FIGURE 10-22:
A wide angle view
is the favorite of
professional
street
photographers.

FIGURE 10-23:
Both the chef
and the VW
have right-to-left
visual flow.

Visual flow, or a sense of direction, is an important compositional consideration for street photographers. When possible, try to compose your scene conscious of the fact that your viewer would like to explore your photo within a certain direction. Maybe that will be from left to right, from top to bottom, or a winding S-shaped curve through a garden path. Visual flow allows your viewers to appreciate the picture space and often encourages them to imagine themselves within your photographic scene.

Avoiding faces to maintain anonymity

With all the tips and tricks contained in the chapter, one overriding principle is to follow your ethical principles when you capture people on the streets. If you have any qualms about doing street photography, you can simply capture urban scenes with no faces visible. Take a look at Figure 10-24, which shows an example of a classic street photo scene. The person's anonymity is retained, but not at the expense of the photo's artistry.

FIGURE 10-24:
Privacy is retained in this iPhone street photo.

Street photography snobs may try to convince you that faces need to be in the shot. This is not true, and you should never feel less creative by choosing to avoid faces if that is what you are comfortable with. There will always be interesting ways to capture people on the streets that avoid faces, such as the man carrying a tire on his head in Figure 10-25.

FIGURE 10-25: An iPhone street photo that is both creative and unobtrusive.

3

Editing, Organizing, and Sharing Your Photos

IN THIS PART . . .

Edit with the iOS Photos app.

Organize your photos like a pro.

Share your photos.

Chapter **11**

Editing with the iOS Photos App

n this chapter, I show you around the iOS Photos app, which is the home of your photo-editing tools.

REMEMBER

Please keep in mind that at the time of this writing, the 11 series iPhones have a different look and set of options than some earlier model iPhones. If you're using an earlier model iPhone, most of what you encounter in this chapter is still applicable to you. However, a few added features are accessible only with later series iPhones.

Opening Your Photos App

When new iPhone photographers take their first photo, they often access their photos directly from their iPhone's Camera app. However, when you're not taking pictures, you can access your photo collection faster using the iOS app called Photos.

The Photos app comes with all iPhones and is both the storage location for each image you take and the home of your photo-editing tools. You can access the Photos app by tapping the icon shown in Figure 11-1.

FIGURE 11-1:
The Photos
app has a
multicolored
flower
appearance,
and comes with
all iPhones.

TIP

If you're new to the Photos app, you can skip a lot of confusion by going straight to a section called Albums. After you tap on the Photos app icon, you see a screen similar to Figure 11-2. Tap Albums for an ordered listing of your photos.

FIGURE 11-2:
Tap Albums to
quickly access
your entire image
collection.

Recents is the first album at the top left of your screen. In Figure 11-2, the Recents album contains a photo of a red door. If you're wondering about the albums called Japan Workshop and Jerusalem Workshop, I custom-created these albums to help organize my photos. (To find out how to create your own extra albums, go to Chapter 12.)

When you tap on the Recents album, you see a layout similar to Figure 11-3. The last photo at the bottom right of your screen is usually the last one that you took. For example, the photo with the red door in Figure 11-3 was the most recent photo taken. All the other photos were captured prior to the red door photo.

Exploring Your Editing Options

You can edit any of the photos in the Recents album by tapping it. When you do, you see a layout similar to the one shown in Figure 11-4. When you're ready to edit, tap the word Edit at the top right of your screen.

Starting with Auto adjustments

Your first editing option is called Auto. If the camera club snobs tell you that you can't use the Auto adjustment feature, ignore them! The Auto option, shown in Figure 11-5, is what your iPhone thinks is best for your photo. Is your iPhone's judgment always correct? No . . . but it's pretty smart at guessing what is best for your photo. Tap on the magic wand icon to see what your iPhone comes up with.

FIGURE 11-4:
Access your editing tools via the Edit icon at the top right of your screen.

FIGURE 11-5:
When you tap Auto, your iPhone will judge what it thinks are the best editing tools for your photo.

TIP

When you're starting out on your great editing journey, it's often helpful to see what your iPhone thinks is best. By studying the editing results of your iPhone, you'll get a sense of what the iPhone does right, and what it doesn't do right, based on your own particular tastes.

Getting to know the editing tools

In addition to tapping the Auto button (see preceding section), you can edit your photo manually. Your iPhone offers quite a few editing tools.

Exposure

The Exposure tool is immediately to the right of your Auto icon. Exposure is probably the tool beginner editors use the most because it's quick and easy. The Exposure slider starts at 0, and can be adjusted to a very dark –100 or a very bright +100.

Figure 11-6 shows a visual snippet of what happens when you increase exposure from 0 to 75. The photo gets brighter as the number increases. Conversely, the photo would get darker as you adjust the Exposure slider to the left.

FIGURE 11-6:
Increasing exposure from 0 to 75.

Exposure is a simple and effective method for getting quick results when your photo was too bright or too dark to begin with. In time, however, you may want to stop using Exposure and rely on the other more accurate tools, such as Highlights, Shadows, and Black Point.

Brilliance

The best way to describe the Brilliance tool is to compare it to the Exposure tool. When you increase the exposure in an image, eventually the light areas of the photo will become *blown-out* (far too bright). Interestingly, if you slide the Brilliance tool all the way up to 100, the white areas don't become blown-out and remain acceptably exposed.

The Brilliance tool selectively adjusts certain tonal aspects of your photo while protecting other tones so that your photo doesn't end up looking like a mess.

TIP

Use this tool for a fast way to increase the exposure of your image while retaining highlight details. This tool doesn't adjust your photo's color saturation.

Highlights

The Highlights tool adjusts the light-toned areas of your photo while ignoring and not adjusting the middle and dark tones of your image. This tool is helpful for rescuing photos that have gray or muddy looking highlight areas that in real life should look much whiter.

Give this tool a try, sliding from the negative to the positive side. Do you notice that only the bright parts of the image are being adjusted?

Shadows

The opposite adjustment of the Highlights tool, the Shadow adjustment slider affects only the darker areas of your photo.

You may find yourself using this tool to make your shadows a bit brighter to see the full picture better or to decrease the shadows for a more dramatic, fine art look.

Contrast

The Contrast tool gives your photo a bit more punch, especially if you feel that the overall look of your photo is murky or soft looking. The Contrast tool will make all shadow and black aspects of your photo even darker, and all highlight and white aspects will become even whiter.

WARNING

Be careful not to overuse this tool. It's okay in small doses, but you'll be better served to learn how to use the other tools for selective tonal adjustments.

This tool isn't used very much by pros because it often goes overboard with the highlight areas of your photo.

Brightness

The Brightness tool could be loosely described as a more powerful and accurate Exposure tool. Try adjusting your photo with the Exposure tool and then compare the effects of what happens when you make adjustments with your Brightness tool.

Brightness adjusts your photo to the brighter side while not allowing the very bright areas to become blown-out and useless. When you adjust your photo to the extreme using the Exposure tool, the light-toned areas became pure white and ugly.

Black Point

The Black Point tool is a favorite for fine art, street, and fashion photographers. By adjusting the slider to the negative side, all very dark areas of your photo will become a muddy gray mess. Not good! But try the slider adjustment to the right. Now you have some magic.

TIP

Use the Black Point tool to add drama to your photos. Added drama is easily accomplished when the shadow areas of your photo become darker and darker. Keep in mind that you probably won't want to use this tool heavily when you're wanting to show a sense of peace, calm, relaxation, or if you're doing wedding or family photography.

Extreme Black Point adjustments are more for gritty and bold photos that are meant to shake things up.

Saturation

The Saturation tool adjusts all colors in your photo, either with more color boost or less color. If you go to the minus side, your colors will fade to black and white. If you go to the plus side of the slider, your photos will become a very garish mess of super-saturated color. Use this tool sparingly!

Vibrance

You can consider the Vibrance tool a smarter version of the Saturation tool. Vibrance adjustments tend to boost the color intensity of areas that are not origi-nally oversaturated while ignoring the areas that are already saturated enough.

The Vibrance tool also tends to protect people's skin tone, keeping a boost of vibrance from making their skin look unnaturally oversaturated.

Warmth

The Warmth tool adjusts your photo to a more bluish color cast on the minus side and a warm, yellow-toned look when adjusted to the plus side.

TIP

Landscapes and nature look great with warm tones, and moody, dramatic photos often look better with a cool blue tone.

Tint

The Tint tool adjusts your photo between the green and magenta color spectrum.

TIP

If you feel that your photo is too green due to old tube-style fluorescent light bulbs, simply go to the magenta side of the adjustment slider to correct the color balance of your photo.

Sharpness

Late model iPhones usually don't need much image sharpening. However, if you feel that your photo is just not as sharp as you'd like, this adjustment slider can give your photo an extra sharpness boost.

Definition

The Definition tool is a clever method of adding drama to your photos. It acts as a sort of middle-tone contrast adjustment, which allows for a contrasty appearance while not ruining your highlight areas.

TIP

Use this tool for your black-and-white photo, plus any image that needs a hit of fine-art drama. This filter should probably not be used in excess for weddings, baby photography, or happy-looking family portraits. It's used more for a gritty, tough look.

Noise Reduction

The Noise Reduction tool is almost irrelevant with the very advanced iPhone 11 series. If you have an earlier model iPhone and you feel that your photo has too much of what is often called *grain,* then this slider can help remove those digital dots that detract from photos taken in low light.

The iPhone 11 series has Night mode activated by default, which uses complex processing to remove noise from each of your photos. You may, therefore, not find the Noise Reduction tool useful if you're using an 11 series or later iPhone.

Vignette

The Vignette tool adds a soft white border around your photo when the adjustment slider is taken to the left and a dark soft border when slid to the right.

TIP

The white vignettes have been popular in decades past for wedding and family photography, and the black vignette looks great with gritty black-and-white street and portrait photographs.

Applying Filters

Filters are a quick and easy way for you to add a sense of drama and artistry to your image. A *filter* is a mixture of color and tonal adjustments created by software and app developers to help enhance the look of your photos. When you apply a filter, you will see an immediate change to your photo, with some filters looking great and some filters looking ridiculous. While it's true that filters are often overused, you can dial back some of the extreme effects of filter usage for a more subtle approach.

To apply a filter, tap on the little icon at the bottom center of your screen. The icon looks like three overlapping circles and is shown in Figure 11-7. The first highlighted option is called ORIGINAL, which simply means that no changes have been made to your photo. Other filters appear to the right of the original photo.

Vivid

To the right of ORIGINAL is a filter titled VIVID. Tap on that version of your photo, and you'll no doubt see your colors pop, and the overall photo will become more *visually present* (a fancy term for punchier colors and a grand lack of subtlety).

Figure 11-8 shows an example of how the palm ferns have a more aggressive color intensity than the Figure 11-7 sample.

TIP

Use the Vivid filter for scenes that require an over-the-top amount of color saturation and punch. Landscapes, nature, and gardens are great subjects for Vivid filter usage.

FIGURE 11-7:
Access Filters by tapping on the icon with three overlapping circles at the bottom center of your screen.

FIGURE 11-8:
The Vivid filter boosts color saturation and shadow areas.

Vivid Warm

Vivid Warm is the name of the filter that adds a measure of yellow and orange to the Vivid appearance. A lot of fine art color iPhone photographers use this warmer toned filter to replicate slide film from the 1960s and '70s.

Compare Figure 11-9 with Figure 11-8. The colors are still punchy, but the warm tones really boost the mood.

Vivid Cool

Instead of the yellow and orange look of the Vivid Warm option, the Vivid Cool filter has a blue color cast added to it.

REMEMBER

More blue added to a photo sometimes imparts a feeling of loneliness and alienation, but at other times, the blue-toned look adds an element of fine art to your color images.

Dramatic

The Dramatic filter produces a similar result as the Definition tool. There isn't much color change, but rather an attractive middle-tone contrast increase. This midtone contrast has the effect of adding a more graphic, artistic look, changing the photo from a snapshot to a more intentionally artistic work.

Dramatic Cool

The Dramatic Cool filter is similar to the Dramatic filter, but you see a bluish color added to your photo.

TIP

Use this filter for moody street scenes where you'd rather have a sense of tension in your photo than a sense of relaxation.

Mono

Out of the three black-and-white filters, Mono is the most normal-looking black and white. Similar to reducing the Saturation slider to -100, Mono removes the color from your photo to produce a good looking standard black-and-white image.

REMEMBER

Don't feel nervous about turning your color photo to black and white. If you keep your photo within your iOS Photos app, you can switch back to a color photo any time you'd like, even years from now.

Silvertone

The Silvertone filter is a pleasant throwback to classic black-and-white film processing. Your photo will have a silvery sheen added to it, which can look great for certain applications, such as printing and framing.

Noir

The Noir filter gives your photos a rich, dark, shadowy look, reminiscent of mid-century *Film Noir* Hollywood movies. Use this filter for emotion-laden fine art portraits or street photography.

While the Noir filter looks very cool, sometimes you may want a less intense version of the filter's look. No problem!

TIP

Figure 11-10 shows the Noir filter, but only applied at 65 percent strength. After you apply any filter, simply play around with the intensity slider to dial in the amount of the filter that you like. As you can see, the 65 Noir filter amount pulls back a bit of the color but still retains some of the Noir appearance.

FIGURE 11-10: Reduce the intensity of any filter using the intensity slider underneath each filter.

Cropping an Image

TIP

Cropping your photo is an effective way to concentrate the viewer's attention to the most important part of your photo. To crop an image simply means that you're cutting away at least one side of your four-sided rectangular or square photograph.

Professional photographers use cropping all the time. If any parts of the photo have a visual distraction or are nonessential, they'll often just crop the image to get rid of the distraction. You can do the same!

Using (and disabling) the Auto Crop tool

Auto Crop is a feature that intelligently scans your photo and alters it slightly for perfect straightness and perspective. Auto cropping occurs when you tap on the crop tool icon at the bottom of your screen, as shown in Figure 11-11. If you like the straightening that your iPhone suggests, then you don't need to do anything else.

FIGURE 11-11:
Auto cropping occurs if your iPhone thinks that your photo may not be straight or needs perspective adjustments.

But what if you don't like your iPhone's straightening suggestion? No problem! Simply tap the little yellow icon at the top middle of your screen to revert to the original non-auto rotated image. The yellow-colored Done word at the bottom always accept your edits and takes you to the finished photo. You can go back and re-edit your photo as many times as you like.

Flipping your image horizontal

While you'll rarely need to flip your image horizontally, Figure 11-12 shows you the icon to use if you need a type of mirrored-image look.

FIGURE 11-12:
Create a mirrored
image effect by
using the Flip
Horizontal tool.

Rotating your photo 90 degrees

A 90-degree rotation can be helpful for abstract images. If you photographed a nonrecognizable object horizontally but wanted a vertical for framing on the wall, use the 90-degree rotation tool (see Figure 11-13). You may also want to add the Flip Horizontal tool in tandem with the 90-degree rotation for extra abstract effects.

FIGURE 11-13:
Use the Rotate
tool to create
abstract sideways
or upside-down
photos.

Adjusting Aspect Ratio

The term *Aspect Ratio* can best be described as the length and width dimension parameters that force your photo to fit into a specific frame.

For example, what if you went to your local camera store and got a 3-x-4 inch print made, but your desktop frame called for a 4-x-6 aspect ratio instead? With aspect ratio adjusting, you can prepare your photo to conform to the appropriate aspect ratio based on your photo frame size.

This aspect ratio adjustment doesn't permanently change your photo, as you can always go back to the original aspect ratio at any time. As in Figure 11-14, you can use the following aspect ratio presets to crop your photo to fit specific frame sizes.

>> **ORIGINAL:** This option retains the aspect ratio of the original photo that you took prior to any editing.

>> **FREEFORM:** This option allows you unhindered cropping and aspect ratio adjustment.

>> **SQUARE:** This option will give you a perfectly square crop (aspect ratio).

>> **16:9 Horizontal, 9:16 Vertical:** Choose 16:9 for photos to be placed within a video or movie.

- » **10:8 Horizontal, 8:10 Vertical:** This aspect ratio is one of the most common for wall-hung frames.

- » **7:5 Horizontal, 5:7 Vertical:** This is also a common frame and matte size for hanging smaller photos on the wall.

- » **4:3 Horizontal, 3:4 Vertical:** This is the default aspect ratio for iPhone cameras.

- » **5:3 Horizontal, 3:5 Vertical:** A rarely used aspect ratio.

- » **3:2 Horizontal, 2:3 Vertical:** North America's most common print size is a 4x6 inch print, which is a 2:3 aspect ratio. This is also a common aspect ratio for DSLR and mirrorless style cameras.

If you don't like the results of your aspect ratio cropping, you can move the picture around within the aspect ratio frame by swiping your photo in any direction that you choose.

FIGURE 11-14:
Aspect ratio presets fit common photo mattes and frames.

TIP

Even though the terms *crop* and *aspect ratio* are technically not the same, people often use those terms to describe the same thing. Someone might say, for example, "I prefer a 16:9 crop for my photos." They could also say, "I prefer a 16:9 aspect ratio for my photos."

Cropping a photo is an action that you do, and a photo's aspect ratio is the length by width relationship of any rectangle or square.

Editing Your Portrait Photography

In Chapter 4, you discover how to use Portrait mode on yourself, creating dynamic selfies that really stand out. But did you know that you can re-edit your portrait photos long after you take them?

To re-edit your Portrait mode photo, simply locate it in your normal iOS Photos app, which is sometimes referred to as your *camera roll*.

TIP

A shortcut to your Portrait mode photos is to scroll down within your Photos app until you see a heading called Media Types, as in Figure 11-15. By tapping on the word Portrait, you won't need to endlessly wade through all your camera roll photos and videos to find your portrait.

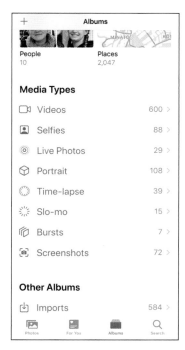

FIGURE 11-15:
Access all your Portrait mode photos within a dedicated portrait folder.

When you photograph a friend using Portrait mode, the background blur amount often defaults to what is called *f4.5*. Your iPhone chooses the default amount of background blur, as it assumes that its choice is artistically best. However, the following steps show you how to add a bit more background blur.

Not all iPhones have Portrait mode. If none of what is shown in the following steps looks familiar to you, your iPhone doesn't have Portrait mode.

1. **Choose your Portrait mode photo and tap Edit at the top right of your screen.**

2. **Tap the f-number, as shown in Figure 11-16.**

FIGURE 11-16:
Tap the f-number.

3. **Place your finger on the DEPTH scroll wheel, as shown in Figure 11-17.**

4. **Scroll horizontally until the f-number is as low as possible, as in Figure 11-18.**

5. **When you have the maximum background blur behind the person, tap Done.**

When your background is as blurred as you want it to be, you can continue editing with various backgrounds, filters, and manual adjustments.

FIGURE 11-17:
The DEPTH scroll
wheel affects the
amount of
background blur.

FIGURE 11-18:
When the
f-number is as
low as possible,
you will see
maximum
background blur.

IN THIS CHAPTER

» **Updating your settings**

» **Favoriting your best photos**

» **Organizing your albums**

» **Searching for people and places**

» **Sorting your files for media types**

» **Using the search tool**

Chapter **12**

Organizing and Sharing Your Photos like a Pro

One of the greatest frustrations that photography instructors and photo workshop leaders hear about is "I love taking photos, but I have thousands of images and they are spread out everywhere! I need a logical and efficient workflow."

If this statement describes you, or possibly you in the future, then you can benefit from this chapter, which shows you how to get yourself into an organized post-production photography workflow.

Thinking about Post-Production Workflow

The term *post-production workflow* is often used in photography circles and refers to what you do with your image the moment after you take the photo.

After you take your photo, you have several options:

>> Place it in an album.

>> Edit it (see Chapter 11).

>> Delete it, if necessary.

>> Mark it as a favorite.

>> Share it with other people or on social media.

Deleting Unwanted Photos

Do you have any fear of hitting the Delete button? Most photographers do, especially when they realize that they deleted when in a bad mood.

Don't ever delete photos when you're tired, hungry, frustrated, or in a bad mood. Delete unwanted photos when you're in the groove! You'll have far better objectivity when you purge your images coming from a good mindset. You want to delete photos based on a few parameters:

>> You have duplicate photos that are pretty much identical to each other.

>> You really dislike the photo and realize that no editing magic will save it from the trash can.

>> You're concerned about filling up your iPhone and/or iCloud allotment with sub-par photos.

For many photographers, it's the last one in the preceding list that drives the decision to purge unwanted photos. If you have an iCloud account, you'll eventually surpass your 5GB of free cloud storage space. If you don't want a monthly subscription to purchase extra iCloud storage, you'll want to keep your photo and video collection purged of unnecessary photos and videos.

It's a good idea to schedule a monthly purge session at your favorite café. Get comfortable with a tasty drink, and as you're in a great mood, you'll have the objectivity to delete photos that really won't serve you in the future. Keeping your collection clean and organized each month (at the least) is part of an efficient photographer's workflow.

Deleting a photo

The following steps walk you through the process of deleting one of your photos:

1. **Go to Albums view within your Photos app.**

    You can tell your Albums view because it appears in blue at the bottom of the screen (see Figure 12-1).

2. **Go to the Recents folder and tap on the photo that you'd like to delete (refer to Figure 12-1).**

3. **When your photo pops up full-screen, tap the trash can icon at the bottom right, as shown in Figure 12-2.**

    A warning message appears.

FIGURE 12-2:
When tapped, the
trash can icon will
delete your
photo.

4. **Tap on Delete Photo if you want to continue with the deletion (see Figure 12-3).**

You're given a choice to Delete Photo or to Cancel.

The photo disappears from the Recents album.

Recovering a deleted photo

REMEMBER

After you delete a photo, you have 30 days to rescue it from the trash can if you so desire. Otherwise, on day 31, that particular photo will be deleted forever. While not completely necessary, some photographers like to scan their trash can once in a while just to make sure they didn't delete a photo prematurely. This practice is completely up to you, and may or may not be helpful.

Follow these steps to retrieve your lost gems:

1. **At the bottom of your screen, tap the icon called Albums twice.**

You return to the All Albums screen.

FIGURE 12-3:
Choose Delete
Photo to proceed
with the deletion.

2. **Scroll all the way to the bottom of that page until you see Recently Deleted, which is located in the Other Albums section.**

   You see an album of photos that are in the queue to be deleted. The red text at the bottom of each photo thumbnail tells you when that particular photo will be deleted.

3. **Search for the photo that you wrongly deleted and tap on it.**

4. **At the bottom right of your screen, tap on the word Recover.**

   Your photo reappears in your Recents album.

Favoriting Photos with the Heart Icon

Larger photo management software, such as Lightroom, allows for multistar ratings and flagging, which are tools used by photographers to assign value to an image. Your iOS Photos app has a simplified but still useful evaluative tool called the *heart*, also known as a *favorite*.

When you *heart* a photo, you're placing a certain value on that photo based on whatever parameters that you ascribe to it. For example, maybe you hearted all your favorite photos because they're all destined to be uploaded to your Instagram page. Or maybe all your hearted photos are singled out because you want to print each one of them.

Regardless of why you tapped the heart icon, the fact that you have the ability to single out one or many photos for a future end-use is convenient.

To apply the heart to your favorite photos, simply open your photo and tap on the little heart icon at the bottom of your screen, as shown in Figure 12-4.

FIGURE 12-4:
The heart icon is below the photo that you want to favorite.

TIP

You can find all your hearted favorites in your My Albums area within the Albums section. Figure 12-5 shows an example of where you can find the Favorites folder, which is directly under the Recents folder. In Figure 12-5, you can see that 242 photos have the heart icon tapped.

FIGURE 12-5:
The Favorites
folder holds all of
your *hearted*
images.

There is no limit to how many hearts you can apply, nor is there any minimum. Some photographers don't even bother using the heart tool at all.

Diving into Album Organization

Organizing your photos may seem like a pain and a waste of time, but if you get in the habit of placing every photo within a custom named album, your future self will greatly thank you for it.

You can find all of your photos in the Recents folder. The Recents folder is the master folder that contains all the photos that you've taken with your iPhone's camera and/or have imported from external cameras or devices.

REMEMBER

The term Recents is not completely accurate because you can find your whole history of photos in it. However, the name Recents is as good a name as any, as it quickly shows you the most recent photos you've taken or imported.

Selecting photos to create a new album

Your iOS Photos app lets you create as many albums as you like, which keeps your photo collection organized. To discover how to quickly create and populate a new album, follow these easy steps:

1. **Within your Recents album, tap on the word Select.**

2. **Tap several photos to create a sample Album.**

   At this point, it doesn't matter which photos you select.

3. **When you see little blue check marks on each photo that you tapped (see Figure 12-6), tap the little up-arrow Share icon at the bottom left of your screen.**

4. **At the bottom of the new screen, tap on the words Add to Album.**

   You're prompted to create a new album.

5. **Tap on the words New Album and name your new album.**

   Your newly created album now contains your selected photos. You can access this album from within My Albums.

Removing a photo from an album

Deleting a photo and removing a photo from your album are not the same thing. When you remove a photo from an album, you're not deleting your photo. You're just removing it from that particular album that you are viewing. The photo will still be visible with your Recents album.

Follow these steps to remove photos from an album:

1. **Within your album, tap the Select option at the top right of your screen.**

2. **Tap on the photo that you want to remove from your sample album.**

3. **Tap on the words Remove from Album, as shown in Figure 12-7.**

REMEMBER

   Removing a photo from your album doesn't delete your photo. It only removes it from the album. If you want to delete the photo entirely, simply tap the word Delete. To rescue a photo that you deleted by mistake, go to your Recently Deleted folder located at the bottom of your Albums section.

FIGURE 12-7: Remove from Album doesn't delete your photo. It just removes it from the album.

Using albums wisely

Here's the most important organizational tip: Every photo should have its own album!

One of the biggest complaints that beginner and amateur photographers have is not being able to find a specific photo quickly. You can save so much time by placing each photo that you take or import into an album. In fact, every photo that's in your Recents album should have a home within a custom-created folder with a logical naming structure.

Here are some common folder name ideas that make sense for organizing your entire photo collection:

>> Italy Trip 2020

>> Grandchildren

>> Business receipts

>> House ideas

>> Nature photos

>> Hockey games

The names of the albums are completely up to you. Even though placing every photo in an album may seem like a lot of work, it's actually a timesaver in the long run as you will have very quick access to each photo in the future.

Finding photos of a single person

The People feature within People & Places of the Albums section is a great way for you to quickly find most or all photos of a single person. Using clever facial recognition, this feature shows you all photos of you and then all photos of other friends or family members. Your iPhone uses artificial intelligence to categorize the people who you photograph most, including yourself.

The Places feature uses location data to determine what city and country your photos were taken in. This feature usually works only for mobile device cameras, such as iPhones and Android devices, and less so for larger cameras, such as DSLRs and mirrorless-style cameras.

The People & Places feature is just another great way for you to quickly access photos that previously would take a lot of scrolling to find. Being a good iPhone photographer is one thing, but the complete photography workflow also includes quick access to your entire photo collection. With this and other search tools, you will be well-positioned to access your photographic history quickly.

Sorting your files by media types

The Media Types area (within the Albums section) is a quick way for you to access certain types of media files. Here's a brief description of each search parameter, illustrated in Figure 12-8:

» **Videos:** A collection of all videos that you've filmed

» **Selfies:** Each selfie that you've taken of yourself with the front-facing selfie camera

» **Live Photos:** The location of all Live Photos (they look like mini video clips)

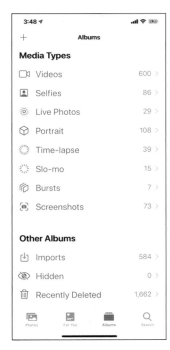

FIGURE 12-8: The Media Types section helps you quickly search for only certain types of media files.

- >> **Portrait:** Each photo with Portrait mode turned on

- >> **Time-lapse:** All videos created with sped-up motion

- >> **Slo-mo:** Your slow-motion video collection

- >> **Bursts:** Each photo that you shot with Burst mode

- >> **Screenshots:** Photos (screen captures) of your iPhone screen

Using the Other Albums section

The last three options within the Other Albums section are:

- >> **Imports:** A collection of all photos that were not taken with your iPhone's camera. This collection is usually populated with photos that you've imported from your larger DSLR or mirrorless-style cameras.

- >> **Hidden:** A collection of photos that you've hidden to keep private. You can hide any photo by selecting that photo, choosing the up-arrow Share icon, and then tapping the Hide option. Hiding photos is useful for when you do public slideshows using your Photos collection, but don't want anyone seeing certain images.

- >> **Recently Deleted:** The location of all photos that you've deleted within the last 30 days. You can retrieve photos from the trash can, but after 30 days, they will be deleted forever.

Knowing When to Use the Photos Section

You can access the Photos section from the bottom left of your screen, as shown in Figure 12-9. This section, which includes date-based image searching features, is another excellent tool to quickly access only certain photos based on when they were captured.

- >> **Years:** Search for all photos within a certain year only.

- >> **Months:** Search for month-specific photos.

- >> **Days:** Access photos from certain days of the week.

- >> **All photos:** See and select all your photos within a zoomed view; tap on the +/- icon at the top right of this screen for different zoomed viewing options.

Making the For You Section Work, Well, for You

Figure 12-10 shows an example of what your For You section looks like. For You is a very feature-rich section that is yet another tool for quick image searching, but also artificial intelligence-based suggestions to make your photos look even better.

You can access this section by tapping on the icon at the bottom of your screen.

Try out the following features that allow for advanced photo and video searching as well as automated effect editing suggestions:

» **Sharing Suggestions:** Based on facial recognition, suggestions of photos that you may want to share with certain friends and family.

» **Memories:** Photos and videos of your best memories based on location and also artificial intelligence. This section is great for slideshows at family get-togethers!

>> **Featured Photos:** Images that your iPhone thinks you will like the best based on the quality of the photo and the subject matter.

>> **Effect Suggestions:** Suggestions on how you can make your photos look better. You can accept or ignore these editing suggestions.

>> **Shared Albums:** A grouping of all the shared albums that have been shared both with you and from you.

Using the Search Tool within the Photos App

At the bottom right of your screen is a magnifying glass icon, which is called the Search Tool. By tapping on the magnifying glass, you see even more intelligent suggestions for searching photos based on various parameters:

>> **Moments:** Intelligent searching based on categories given to you, such as One Year Ago, Winter, Trips, Dining, or any other topic that iOS Photos thinks you may be interested in

>> **People:** Albums of the most important people in your photographic life based on facial recognition technology

>> **Places:** City and region photo collections based on location data collected from your iPhone's camera metadata

>> **Categories:** Smart categories created by your iPhone, such as Cars, Snow, Forests, Bicycles, Sports, Food, and so on

>> **Groups:** A facial-recognition based image collection based on photos with common relationship groupings

Sharing Your Photos

Quickly sharing photos of friends and family is one of the great gifts of our time. Grandparents in Vancouver can see same-day photos of their grandchild's birthday party halfway around the world. But emailing large amounts of higher quality photos can be cumbersome, and not everyone wants to share family photos on social media.

Fortunately, you have several ways you can share photos with family and friends and also on social media.

Using shared albums

Shared albums are quite feature-rich. iCloud allows you to easily share a very large number of photos and videos with anyone you choose, anywhere in the world. Your friends can add their own photos to your shared album, and they can comment and like each photo.

TIP

As of this writing, you can share a single album with up to 100 friends! The current cap is 5,000 media files, which refers to a combination of photos and videos.

Follow these steps to send any number of your photos to friends or family members:

1. **Choose the photos you want to send by tapping Select and then selecting all the photos that you want to share.**

2. **Tap the up-arrow at the bottom right.**

3. **Tap the words Add to Shared Album.**

4. **When prompted, create a comment.**

   For example, you might type "6th birthday party pics for Aunt Martha."

5. **Below the comments section, choose to create a New Shared Album and name it with an album title of your choice.**

6. **Add your recipient's email address and then tap the blue-colored Next.**

7. **(Optional) Enter another comment.**

   You don't have to enter anything here. Think of this comment as the message part of an email.

8. **Tap the blue-colored Post.**

   When you return to your normal Albums view, a Shared Albums folder that includes your photos appears.

Figure 12-11 shows an example of my two shared albums. The first one is an album shared to Mark Hemmings from Carrol Bern. You can tell that it was an incoming shared album because of the wording *From* Carrol Bern. The second album, however, was sent from Mark to a number of family members. You can tell that it was an outgoing shared album because of the wording From You.

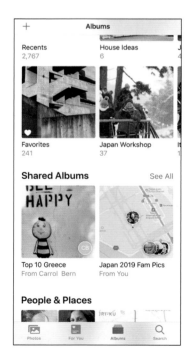

FIGURE 12-11:
Shared Albums is the location for all photos shared to and from you.

Sharing to any location

You can share your awesome photo with others using several different methods. The following list explains the sharing options you can access by going to your Recents folder, tapping Select, and then selecting the photos you want to share:

>> **Airdrop:** By tapping this option, you can send your high-quality photos and videos to a friend's nearby iPhone, iPad, or Mac computer. Make sure both of your devices have Wi-Fi and Bluetooth turned on.

>> **Messages:** This option lets you send your photos through the normal Apple iMessage service. This option works for any iOS or OSX device.

>> **Mail:** When you choose to send your photos through Apple's emailing service called Mail, you're often given the choice of what quality to send the photos. Choose between Small, Medium, or Actual Size.

>> **Notes:** If you like to use your iPhone's Notes app, you'll love being able to easily add any photos or screenshots to your Notes app simply by tapping this option. Choose a new note or an existing note, and your photo will be added within a few seconds.

>> **Reminders:** Following the exact same process as Notes, you can add any photo or screenshot to the Reminders app as well. Choose either a new reminder or an existing reminder.

>> **Other third-party apps:** If you've installed other apps that partner with iOS sharing, you will see them alongside Reminders. Feel free to share your photos to these apps as well. Some common ones are Gmail, Google Drive, Messenger, and Dropbox.

>> **Copy Photos:** Some apps allow for pasting photos. To do so, you can copy your photo(s) with this option and paste them in a different app.

>> **Add to Shared Album:** See the preceding section for a detailed explanation on how to create shared albums.

>> **Add to Album:** Use this option to add new or old photos to any of your custom-created albums. This important tool is keeps your entire collection organized.

>> **Duplicate:** Some iPhone photographers like to make duplicates (copies) of their photos, especially if they need to send two edited versions of the same image. You can duplicate any of your photos by using this tool. Your newly created duplicate photo will show up as the most recent photo taken, within your Recents folder.

>> **Hide:** Are you going to do a public slideshow that includes your Photos app? Or maybe you need to show your photo collection to someone. Hide sensitive photos by using this tool. When you're done showing your photos to the person or people, you can unhide those photos or keep them hidden. You can access

all your hidden photos from within the Other Albums area of the Albums section within the Photos app.

>> **Slideshow:** Select a lot of photos and tap the Slideshow button to show off your images in a fun way. This option works well for projecting onto a TV screen using Apple TV.

>> **Use as Wallpaper:** Choose a photo that you'd like for your iPhone wallpaper. This option works only if you have just one image selected.

>> **Copy iCloud link:** Use this quick and easy way to share one or many photos via iCloud. Choose this option if you want to share videos, as videos are difficult to send through email. When you see the newly created iCloud link, you can send that link to anyone in the world for quick and easy media sharing.

>> **Create Watch Face:** For Apple Watch owners, you can create custom watch faces using your own photos.

>> **Save to Files:** If you're a Files user within iCloud, you can add photos to any iCloud File. The photos sync with your desktop Mac computer's iCloud Drive as well.

>> **Assign to Contacts:** Did you just take a great portrait of your best friend? If so, why not use that photo for their official Contacts bio pic? Contacts is an app on your iPhone that contains all your friend and family contacts.

>> **Print:** If you have a wireless home printer, you can use this option to print your photos.

Sharing to your social media channels

If you post your photos to social media channels, you can quickly share your photos from within the Photos app. Some popular social media sharing options from within Photos are Facebook, Instagram, and Twitter.

To share a photo to one of your social media channels, follow these easy steps:

1. **Select the photo that you want to share.**

2. **Locate the social media app that you want to upload to.**

3. **For Facebook, choose News Feed or Your Story, proceed to describe your photo, and then post it. For Instagram, Twitter, and any other social app, follow their upload instructions.**

TECHNICAL
STUFF

Keep in mind that you won't be able to upload to social media apps unless you've already downloaded those apps prior and also are currently signed in to those apps.

The Part of Tens

Chapter **13**

Ten iOS Apps That Will Enhance Your Photography

Your iPhone is well positioned to offer you a complete photography work-flow. You can take an incredible photo, edit that image, and then, with iCloud's automatic backup, store your photo safely in the cloud.

At times, however, you may find that reaching for another editing tool can help with the creative process. This chapter is designed to give you some of my favorite app suggestions, both free and paid.

Mark's Suggested Free Photography Apps

This section contains five free apps that have proven themselves to be solid cre-ativity enhancers. Some of the following apps have extra premium features that require a purchase, but the free versions listed in the following sections have a lot of useful tools.

Adobe Photoshop Express

The name Photoshop carries a lot of weight, and for good reason. Photoshop is the world leader in photo manipulation, and it spans many creative and business genres. The Express app is full of great features, one of which can help you create montages of your best photos.

With this app, you can take various quantities of your photos to create highly customizable photo montages. The montages come with templates for the major social media channels, and the compositions can be micro-adjusted so that only the best parts of the photos are visible.

Adobe Photoshop Fix

No doubt many times you've encountered a scene where an ugly streak of something ruins the aesthetic. No problem! The Adobe Photoshop Fix app is a free and powerful way to remove those unwanted distractions. This app also works seamlessly with users of the Adobe Lightroom CC app, which is described in the following section.

Adobe Lightroom CC

Lightroom CC is a powerful app that offers its users a complete photographer's workflow. You can take a photo with its in-app camera, edit the photo to perfection, and then upload it to the Adobe Creative Cloud for safekeeping and mobile access.

One could argue that both Apple's iCloud and Adobe's Creative Cloud are competing workflow solutions. Both have similar start-to-finish workflow tools. However, Lightroom CC's editing tools are usually considered to be of a higher quality.

REMEMBER

This app is free, but to unlock some premium features, you need to purchase a monthly plan.

Instagram

Instagram wasn't the first camera app to introduce retro-style filters, but it was certainly the one that introduced digital photo filters to the larger world. While Instagram is more of a social media platform than an image editor, it's included in this list because it's free and it does have basic editing capabilities.

Usually photographers apply their own look to their images and then upload to Instagram, bypassing their sometimes overused filter options. However, if you're in a rush to get a photo out the door, Instagram's filters and basic image editing tools will do the trick.

Facetune2

Teens love Facetune2, but the irony is that they don't even need it! Improving skin smoothness is as easy as painting the brush over the face, and Facetune2 looks after the rest.

Some premium features in this app have a fee, but as of this writing, the skin smoothening feature is free.

Mark's Suggested Paid Photography Apps

Not much in life is free, and even most of the free apps have paid versions that offer more features. The following apps require a payment, but you will certainly get your money's worth out of each app's low cost.

TouchRetouch

The TouchRetouch app has similar functionality to the Photoshop Fix app, described earlier in this chapter. However, TouchRetouch is famous for getting rid of power and telephone lines. With its dedicated Line Removal tool, you simply trace over where the line is within the photo, and the app takes care of the rest. This app is worth every penny for that feature alone! However, it does so much more, such as the tools you would expect . . . clone stamping, healing, and object removal.

Use this app when the beauty of the exterior suffers from distracting wires and other objects.

Slow Shutter Cam

Mobile device cameras, such as iPhones and Androids, aren't able to create real slow shutter effects like their larger DSLR and mirrorless siblings. While the larger cameras can make waterfalls soft and silky due to a slow shutter speed, iPhones need to rely on digital solutions. The Slow Shutter Cam app is a long-standing success story of how app designers can mimic the effects of slow shutter using a digital process. Yes, you get a fake slow shutter photo, but what does fake mean anyway? If it looks good, it matters very little if it was created from an analog process or a digital process.

The app allows you to choose your long exposure in increments of seconds, which gives you a lot of creative freedom on how you want your finished product to look. When you are done with your first image, go straight into the editing tools within the app to adjust saturation and brightness.

Brushstroke

If you want some new wall art in your house or maybe a lovely gift for a friend's birthday, why not transform your favorite photo into what appears to be a painting? After choosing your paint type and variation, you can further adjust the look of your painting by altering the canvas texture or use different mediums altogether. When done, simply print your newly created painting and frame it for your wall!

SKRWT

The odd but intriguingly named SKRWT app is well respected in mobile photography circles as a go-to solution for creating straight architectural photos. Have you ever noticed that when you point your iPhone upward, the building that you are photographing appears to be falling backward? You can remedy this perspective problem quickly using the excellent SKRWT perspective control tools.

LensFlare

If you need to add some warmth to your evening photos, why not digitally illuminate all the electric lights? By using the filter called Sol Invictus within the LensFlare app, you can add multiple layers of various lens flares and lights to create a really fun photo. While it may not look 100 percent realistic, if applied sparingly, you can make your lamps appear quite realistic.

Chapter **14**

Ten Tips for Shooting and Sharing Video with Your iPhone

Your iPhone's Camera app has a lot of extra gems to give you many more ways to express yourself. In this chapter, you discover new ways to use video capture to record the most important people and events in your life. Enjoy!

Accessing the Video Camera within the Photos App

Accessing the video camera couldn't be easier! Open your camera app as if you were going to take a normal photo. To the immediate left of the PHOTO wording, tap VIDEO. When you are ready, tap on the large red shutter button to start recording.

Holding Your iPhone Properly for Smooth Video Recording

Your iPhone has a remarkably good internal stabilizing system. Even though your iPhone does well with steady video, it's always best to do your part to add even more steadiness, simply by holding your phone properly. Keep your arms tight to the rib cage and the iPhone as close to your upper body as possible (but still being able to see the screen).

If you have the budget, a battery powered gimble, such as the excellent DJI Osmo Mobile 3, can give you even more video stability. A *gimble* is a battery-powered stabilizer for your iPhone, and its usage is explained in detail in Chapter 4.

Trimming the Length of Any Video

When you create a video, you may want to get rid of the starting point and/or the ending point of the video to get rid of useless video footage. To tighten-up your video clip, follow these easy steps.

1. Within your Photos app, go to the Albums section.

2. Scroll down until you see the words Media Types.

3. Tap on Videos.

4. Locate the video you want to trim.

5. Tap on the word Edit at the top right of your screen.

6. Pull the edges of your clip to the desired video start point.

7. Do the same if you want to trim the tail-end of your video clip.

8. Press the Play button to review the timing of your trimmed video clip.

9. If you like the trimmed clip, tap the yellow colored Done at the bottom right.

10. Tap Save Video if you don't want to keep the original longer clip or tap Save Video as New Clip if you want to keep both the original clip and the trimmed clip.

Adjusting the Exposure and Filter Settings

Your Photos app allows you to adjust exposure settings and also put filter effects onto your videos. In fact, the process for adjusting exposure and adding filters to video is pretty much the same as how you would edit your normal still photos. (For details, see Chapter 11.)

Tap on the little icon that looks like a clock, and you will then have access to the same editing and filter options that you discover in Chapter 11. Apply popular adjustments, such as contrast, exposure, highlights, and saturation, to make your photo your own.

The Photo filters are useful as you can create a common look that spans both your normal still photos and your motion videos. To access your filters, tap on the little icon that looks like three interconnected circles, which is next to the clock icon.

Cropping Your Video

When you start using your iPhone's video camera, you may find that your composition is a bit off, most likely due to the learning curve in dealing with motion capture instead of normal still-photo capture. If you feel that you need to tighten up your composition to get rid of some dead space, tap on the crop tool.

The crop tool is the same tool used to crop your photos, and it works in the exact same way. Choose the default ORIGINAL to maintain the original 16:9 aspect ratio.

TIP

While it's true that when you crop video you will lose a bit of resolution (and therefore overall quality), most people wouldn't even recognize quality loss due to the fact that video is often viewed on small screens.

When you are done with your crop, tap on the yellow Done button to accept your changes.

Choosing a Video Aspect Ratio

Video is captured at an aspect ratio of 16:9, which is a common ratio for most Hollywood movies and TVs. Sometimes, however, the common 16:9 aspect ratio is not ideal.

TIP

If your video is meant for Facebook or Instagram advertising, you may want to consider a square 1:1 aspect ratio. Square video for advertising is known to have a higher degree of watchability within those social platforms.

Simply tap on the SQUARE option and then place your square crop anywhere within the video that you like. As with any of these video edits, tap the yellow Done option to accept your changes.

Choosing Vertical or Horizontal Orientation

While vertical videos are not common, they're quite useful for creating Facebook and Instagram Stories. And even though Instagram's IGTV video platform accepts normal horizontal videos, it was originally created as a vertical-only video viewing platform.

You can create vertical videos from your normal horizontal videos by simply tapping on the vertical icon at the left side of your screen (while within the Crop tool). Simply place your vertical crop to the location where your main action is located.

Creating Time-Lapse Photography Video Clips

A *time-lapse video* ends up looking like a normal video, but sped up to show the passing of time very quickly. You can have endless fun creating time-lapse videos with your iPhone. Anything that moves around within your composition will look like a funny animation when you finish your time-lapse and press Play to watch.

Follow these easy steps to create your first time-lapse video:

1. **Rotate your iPhone so that you are holding it horizontally.**

    Within your iOS Camera app, you see the default PHOTO option.

2. **Scroll from PHOTO, passing by VIDEO and SLO-MO, and landing on TIME-LAPSE.**

3. **Press the large red circle to start your time-lapse video.**

4. **Record the scene for about 30 seconds or so, and then stop your video.**

5. **After reviewing your video, try it again, but this time for a full minute.**

TIP

If you have a multilens iPhone you can adjust your lens view to suit your scene.

TIP

As you get better at creating time-lapses, you will see better results by using a tripod or by resting your iPhone on a stable surface while recording. A stable iPhone makes time-lapses much more enjoyable to watch.

Capturing Dramatic Video Clips with Slo-Mo

You can consider the slo-mo feature within your iPhone's Camera app as the opposite of a time-lapse. Any object in motion will appear to be moving incredibly slow. This fantastic tool of self-expression is perfect for sports videography, family video memories of small kids tearing through the house, or a fun dance party.

Try out a slow-mo video by following these easy steps:

1. **Tap on the SLO-MO function, which is between VIDEO and TIME-LAPSE.**

2. **Choose your desired lens view if you have a multilens iPhone.**

3. **Compose your screen as you like and then press the large red button to start recording.**

4. **Record your slo-mo for about six or seven seconds and then stop recording.**

5. **Play back your newly created slo-mo and enjoy the slowed-down slice of life!**

Exporting Your Finished Videos

To share any of your videos, time-lapses, and slow-motion videos, follow these steps.

1. **Locate the video that you want to share.**

2. **Press the little up-arrow Share icon.**

   You see multiple share options.

3. **Tap on any option that best suits your sharing needs.**

Some of the more common sharing options are Mail, AirDrop, Drobox, and Google Drive. Whatever sharing option you have available to you, follow the instructions that the app gives you to complete the sharing process.

Chapter **15**

Ten Extra Editing Features to Jazz Up Your Images

n this chapter, you find a lot more tools for your photo and editing tool belt. Markup is a collection of tools to help add extra information to your images, and Live Photo is a great way to create animated photos that are fun to share.

Adding Notes and Text Using Markup

The Markup tool is a nondestructive editing function that allows you to add text, doodles, and lines to your photos. *Nondestructive* means that you can always delete the Markup additions later on, returning to your original photo. While you may not feel the immediate need to use Markup, the uses are endless. Markup is perfect for any industry that uses photographs to explain a situation.

Say that you took a location-scouting photo of an exterior as a reminder to come back when the light was more dramatic. You can create markup text and doodles as a reminder for the return photo shoot later in the day.

REMEMBER

You can always delete your Markups, which means that you're not permanently damaging any of your marked-up photos.

To add Markup notes to one of your photos, try out these steps:

1. **With your chosen photo open, tap Edit.**

2. **Tap on the little circular icon with three dots at the top right of your vertical screen.**

3. **Tap on Markup.**

4. **Choose one of the markers to create your doodle.**

5. **Tap on the plus sign (+) to access your text editor.**

6. **Add any text with any color, anywhere within your photo.**

7. **Press Done at the top right when you're finished editing.**

Adding Your Signature to Your Photos

While it's true that other third-party apps do a better job at adding signatures to your photos, the built-in signatures tool within Markup will do just fine if you're in a rush. To add your signature within the Markup section, follow these steps.

1. **Tap on the plus (+) sign to reveal the Signature tool.**

2. **Tap on the word Signature.**

3. **At the bottom of your screen, sign your name with your finger or touch pen.**

4. **Tap Clear to try creating your signature again if you didn't like it.**

5. **Tap Done when you're happy with the look of your signature.**

6. **Position and resize your signature to appear anywhere within your photo.**

7. **Change the color of your signature by tapping the black circle at the bottom of your screen.**

8. **Press Done to exit.**

9. **With your signature included, feel free to create further photo edits.**

10. **If you don't want to do any further edits, tap Done.**

Adding Extra Markup Options to Your Photo

The Markup section of your Photos app has a few more tools that you may find useful. For example, you can use the Magnifier tool to magnify any section of your photo for greater clarity. You can also add rectangles, circles, and comic speech bubbles to your photos.

The Markup toolbox is full-featured and ready to help you communicate ideas to your clients, your boss, your friends, or even as a reminder to yourself. Try adding all the Markup tools to a single photo to get used to how they work.

Deleting Your Markups to Return to Your Original Photo

If you didn't duplicate your photo for the sake of adding your Markups, then follow these steps to remove your Markups from your original photo:

1. **Open your Markup photo and tap Edit at the top right.**
2. **Tap Revert at the bottom right to delete your Markups and any photo edits.**

To retain your photo edits but only delete your Markups:

1. **Tap the gray circle with three dots at the top right.**
2. **Tap Markup.**
3. **Tap on any of your Markups and choose Delete.**
4. **Repeat this process until each Markup is deleted and then tap Done.**

Creating and Editing a Live Photo

Apple's Live Photo option is a great tool for photographers who are dealing with fast moving subjects. After a Live Photo is taken, you can then choose the best of a bunch of photos. Think of Live Photo as similar to Burst mode but with the added feature of being able to export the Live Photo as a motion GIF, popular with social media uploaders.

See Chapter 2 for information on creating a Live Photo. The following instructions walk you through choosing the most important image, called a *key photo:*

1. **Tap the circular Live Photo icon at the bottom left, next to the word Cancel.**

2. **Tap on any frame to Make Key Photo, which means the best-looking photo in your opinion.**

3. **Tap the words Make Key Photo to accept your choice of the best-looking image.**

4. **Tap Done to accept your choice and view your newly altered Live Photo.**

Creating a Loop Photo

A Loop Photo alters your Live Photo to create a short video clip of your animation being show as a continuous loop. Social media savvy uploaders use these loops (called *GIF*) to add humor to their social posts.

To create a Loop Photo, follow these steps.

1. **Open your Live Photo in the normal iOS Photos app.**

2. **Tap anywhere within your photo and, with your finger, quickly scroll in an upward direction.**

3. **Tap Loop instead of the default Live.**

    Loop is then activated. You then see a repeating Loop video of your moving object.

Creating a Bounce Photo

A Bounce Photo is similar to a Loop Photo, except that your moving object will first go forward (as normal), but then go backward. In a continuous looped fashion, the moving object keeps going forward, then backward, and then forward again.

Follow these steps to create your Bounce Photo:

1. **Open your Live Photo in the normal iOS Photos app.**

2. **Tap anywhere within your photo and, with your finger, quickly scroll in an upward direction.**

3. **Tap Bounce, instead of Live or Loop.**

   Bounce is then activated. You then see a repeating loop video of your moving object going forward, backward, and then forward again without stopping.

Exporting Your Live, Loop, and Bounce Photos

If you want to export your Live, Loop, or Bounce photos for email or social media uploading, simply press the up-arrow Share icon that is always visible under or over every photo within your iOS Photos app. When you tap it, you have the ability to choose any photo-sharing option that you like.

Here are some technical points to keep in mind when sharing your Live, Loop, and Bounce photos:

» If you email your Live Photo, it will be sent only as a single still photo.

» If you email your Loop or Bounce photo, it will be sent as an animated (motion) GIF file.

Creating a Long Exposure Photo

In Chapter 14, you can see what cool effects you can get with the Slow Shutter Cam app. If your iPhone can create a Live Photo, it can also create a simulated slow shutter photo. This means that the moving subject that was in your Live Photo will be transformed into a streak of light and color.

In the same way as you activated your Loop and Bounce Photos, with your finger, flip upward to reveal your Live Photo Effects options. Instead of tapping on Bounce, tap on the last remaining effect called Long Exposure. You then see the newly created blur effect. Practice this technique with moving cars at dusk within a city environment.

Creating Abstract Photos Using Long Exposure

In this tenth of ten extra tips, you discover an easy way to create frame-worthy wall art. To create an abstract Long Exposure photo, try out these steps:

1. **Find a colorful object to photograph.**

2. **Start rotating your iPhone in a clockwise fashion.**

3. **After two seconds of rotation, tap the shutter button to take the Live Photo.**

   WARNING

   Don't stop rotating your iPhone! Keep rotating it for a few more seconds.

   When you are done with your rotation, you see a normal Live Photo.

4. **With your finger, tap, hold, and flick upward on the photo and then choose Long Exposure.**

   Your abstract photo is created.

5. **Tap Edit to jazz up the colors of your Long Exposure.**

   TIP

   Try taking the Black Point editing option to 100 percent for more drama.

6. **When you're done editing the colors, tap Done to complete your newly created abstract photo.**

Index

L

About the Author

Mark Hemmings is a professional travel and street photographer of more than two decades. His first international photography related trip was in Japan in 1997, and he's been photographing in Japan and around the world annually since then. When not working in his Canadian home city as an architectural and advertising photographer, Mark teaches annual photography workshops in Italy, Jerusalem, Mexico, the Caribbean, and Japan.

In addition to an extensive history with Canon, Nikon, Sony, and Fujifilm DSLR and mirrorless cameras, Mark is an internationally recognized iPhone photographer. His @markhemmings Instagram profile offers almost daily iPhone photography inspiration, created to encourage people from around the world to hone their photographic skills. You can view Mark's full photography portfolio at www.markhemmings.com.

Dedication

To my late grandfather Dyson Thomas who gave me my first camera and who inspired me to become a professional photographer.

Author's Acknowledgments

I would like to thank my editors at Wiley who guided me through this, my first *For Dummies* book. And most importantly, my wonderful wife Sue and daughters Aren and Adrienne who are always very supportive and encouraging. Thanks, family!

Publisher's Acknowledgments

Executive Editor: Steve Hayes

Project Editor: Kelly Ewing

Technical Editor: Mia Ewing

Editorial Assistants: Kelsey Baird, Elizabeth Stilwell

Sr. Editorial Assistant: Cherie Case

Production Editor: Siddique Shaik

Cover Image: Courtesy of Mark Hemmings

Leverage the power

Dummies is the global leader in the reference category and one of the most trusted and highly regarded brands in the world. No longer just focused on books, customers now have access to the dummies content they need in the format they want. Together we'll craft a solution that engages your customers, stands out from the competition, and helps you meet your goals.

Advertising & Sponsorships

Connect with an engaged audience on a powerful multimedia site, and position your message alongside expert how-to content. Dummies.com is a one-stop shop for free, online information and know-how curated by a team of experts.

- Targeted ads
- Video
- Email Marketing
- Microsites
- Sweepstakes sponsorship

20 MILLION PAGE VIEWS **EVERY SINGLE MONTH**

15 MILLION UNIQUE VISITORS PER MONTH

43% OF ALL VISITORS ACCESS THE SITE **VIA THEIR MOBILE DEVICES**

700,000 NEWSLETTER SUBSCRIPTIONS **TO THE INBOXES OF**

300,000 UNIQUE **INDIVIDUALS EVERY WEEK**

# of dummies

Custom Publishing

Reach a global audience in any language by creating a solution that will differentiate you from competitors, amplify your message, and encourage customers to make a buying decision.

- Apps
- Books
- eBooks
- Video
- Audio
- Webinars

Brand Licensing & Content

Leverage the strength of the world's most popular reference brand to reach new audiences and channels of distribution.

For more information, visit dummies.com/biz

PERSONAL ENRICHMENT

Staying Sharp
9781119187790
USA $26.00
CAN $31.99
UK £19.99

Facebook
9781119179030
USA $21.99
CAN $25.99
UK £16.99

Guitar
9781119293354
USA $24.99
CAN $29.99
UK £17.99

Investing
9781119293347
USA $22.99
CAN $27.99
UK £16.99

Beekeeping
9781119310068
USA $22.99
CAN $27.99
UK £16.99

Digital Photography
9781119235606
USA $24.99
CAN $29.99
UK £17.99

Meditation
9781119251163
USA $24.99
CAN $29.99
UK £17.99

Pregnancy
9781119235491
USA $26.99
CAN $31.99
UK £19.99

Samsung Galaxy S7
9781119279952
USA $24.99
CAN $29.99
UK £17.99

iPhone
9781119283133
USA $24.99
CAN $29.99
UK £17.99

Crocheting
9781119287117
USA $24.99
CAN $29.99
UK £16.99

Nutrition
9781119130246
USA $22.99
CAN $27.99
UK £16.99

PROFESSIONAL DEVELOPMENT

Windows 10
9781119311041
USA $24.99
CAN $29.99
UK £17.99

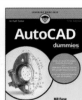

AutoCAD
9781119255796
USA $39.99
CAN $47.99
UK £27.99

Excel 2016
9781119293439
USA $26.99
CAN $31.99
UK £19.99

QuickBooks 2017
9781119281467
USA $26.99
CAN $31.99
UK £19.99

macOS Sierra
9781119280651
USA $29.99
CAN $35.99
UK £21.99

LinkedIn
9781119251132
USA $24.99
CAN $29.99
UK £17.99

Windows 10 All-in-One
9781119310563
USA $34.00
CAN $41.99
UK £24.99

SharePoint 2016
9781119181705
USA $29.99
CAN $35.99
UK £21.99

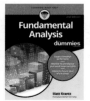

Fundamental Analysis
9781119263593
USA $26.99
CAN $31.99
UK £19.99

Networking
9781119257769
USA $29.99
CAN $35.99
UK £21.99

Office 2016
9781119293477
USA $26.99
CAN $31.99
UK £19.99

Office 365
9781119265313
USA $24.99
CAN $29.99
UK £17.99

Salesforce.com
9781119239314
USA $29.99
CAN $35.99
UK £21.99

Coding
9781119293323
USA $29.99
CAN $35.99
UK £21.99

dummies.com

dummies®
A Wiley Brand

Learning Made Easy

ACADEMIC

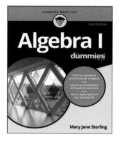

9781119293576
USA $19.99
CAN $23.99
UK £15.99

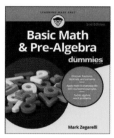

9781119293637
USA $19.99
CAN $23.99
UK £15.99

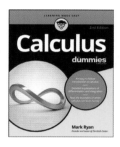

9781119293491
USA $19.99
CAN $23.99
UK £15.99

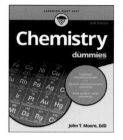

9781119293460
USA $19.99
CAN $23.99
UK £15.99

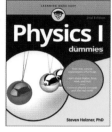

9781119293590
USA $19.99
CAN $23.99
UK £15.99

9781119215844
USA $26.99
CAN $31.99
UK £19.99

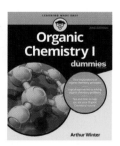

9781119293378
USA $22.99
CAN $27.99
UK £16.99

9781119293521
USA $19.99
CAN $23.99
UK £15.99

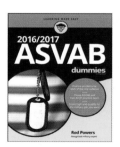

9781119239178
USA $18.99
CAN $22.99
UK £14.99

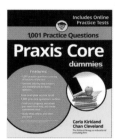

9781119263883
USA $26.99
CAN $31.99
UK £19.99

Available Everywhere Books Are Sold

Small books for big imaginations

9781119177173
USA $9.99
CAN $9.99
UK £8.99

9781119177272
USA $9.99
CAN $9.99
UK £8.99

9781119177241
USA $9.99
CAN $9.99
UK £8.99

9781119177210
USA $9.99
CAN $9.99
UK £8.99

9781119262657
USA $9.99
CAN $9.99
UK £6.99

9781119291336
USA $9.99
CAN $9.99
UK £6.99

9781119233527
USA $9.99
CAN $9.99
UK £6.99

9781119291220
USA $9.99
CAN $9.99
UK £6.99

9781119177302
USA $9.99
CAN $9.99
UK £8.99

Unleash Their Creativity

dummies.com

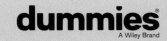